# MAKING SENSE OF ECONOMICS

Ross Chapman was until recently a lecturer in economics at the University of Essex, and at Guelph University, Ontario. He is now lecturing at the University of New South Wales. Juliet Solomon has taught economics in grammar and comprehensive schools and to a variety of adult classes. She is now a lecturer at the Working Men's College of Camden. The illustrator, Steve Lobb, is a lecturer in communication and perception studies, Central London Polytechnic.

# MAKING SENSE OF ECONOMICS

## HOW TO THINK ECONOMICALLY ABOUT DAY-TO-DAY AFFAIRS

*Ross Chapman and Juliet Solomon*

*Illustrated by Steve Lobb*

FONTANA/COLLINS

First published in Fontana 1974
Copyright © Ross Chapman and Juliet Solomon 1974

Made and printed in Great Britain by
Richard Clay (The Chaucer Press), Ltd.,
Bungay Suffolk

# CONTENTS

GOVERNMENT OF IRRESPONSIBLE MONETARY POLICY. THE DEVIL OF INFLATION OR THE DEEP OF UNEMPLOYMENT? Inflation, its causes and remedies – who is to blame for inflation? unions, business, government? more inflation or more unemployment? influence of expectations in different sectors. (Pages 66–78.)

7 STABLE PRICES SEEN AS FIRST AIM OF NEW GOVERNMENT. More about inflation – who loses? who gains? (Pages 79–82.)

8 TRADE FIGURES REVEAL BRITISH FAILURE IN WORLD MARKETS. WORLD DOLLAR SHORTAGE IN THE FIFTIES: GLUT IN THE SEVENTIES. GOVERNMENT STEPS IN TO SAVE THE POUND: RESERVES FALL TO A CRITICAL LEVEL. International trade and exchange rates – why does trade occur? How does it work? Exchange rates, fixed and flexible; currency movements; reserves; problems of exchange mechanism. (Pages 83–93.)

9 BRITAIN MAY BE FORCED TO DEVALUE TO SOLVE BALANCE OF PAYMENTS PROBLEM. STOP-GO POLICIES ARE BACK: SQUEEZE EXPECTED SOON. REPORT RECOMMENDS THE ADOPTION OF FLEXIBLE EXCHANGE RATES. CAN WORLD CURRENCY CRISIS BE AVERTED? The balance of payments problem – current and capital accounts; deficits, policy remedies; devaluation: why it might or might not work; alternatives; more on flexible exchange rates and associated problems. (Pages 94–106.)

10 BRITISH GROWTH RATE ONLY 2% IN 1970. IS 5% FEASIBLE IN 1974? Economic growth – what is it? What causes it? Conflicts with full employment and price stability; inflation, risk and growth. (Pages 107–114.)

11 SHADOW CHANCELLOR QUERIES VALUE OF 'GROWTH AT ALL COSTS'. ENVIRONMENTAL ACTION GROUP SUGGESTS THAT GOVERNMENT SHOULD IMPOSE HEAVY FINES FOR INDUSTRIAL POLLUTION. The environmental problem – how do economists think about pollution? Growth and the distribution of income. (Pages 115–123.)

# TO THE READER

We have written for a person with a latent interest in the workings of the economy but without the time to invest in careful study of a four-hundred-page textbook. Such a reader is unlikely to be helped by the media, which either assume a basic understanding of economic principles or disguise them almost beyond recognition in unhelpful phrases like 'Pound Reels Under Further Speculative Assault'!

Our approach to economic principles is through questions, which are set in the text LIKE THIS, and usually as subheadings. Our answers, *which are set like this*, are not definitive. Unfortunately, in economics only relatively trivial questions invite complete and unqualified answers. Nevertheless, in our answers we demonstrate the method of the economist. We have tried to help the reader to 'think economics' in the context of major current issues.

R.M.C.
J.S.

# 1

# '"WE WILL CUT PRICES AT A STROKE", PRIME MINISTER ANNOUNCES'

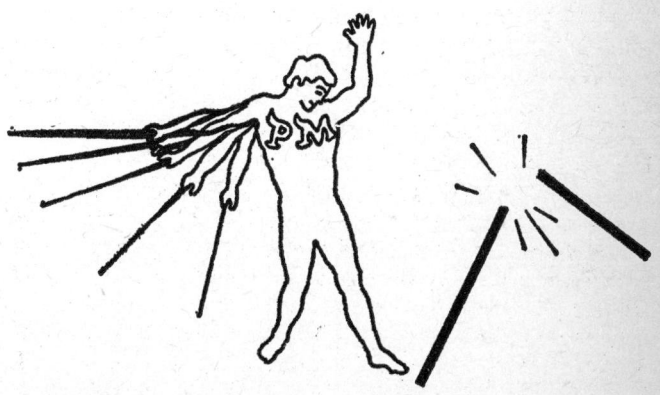

Throughout the western world in the period since the Second World War, all countries have experienced the phenomenon depicted in Figure 1 – that of relentlessly rising prices. While the rate at which the price level has climbed varies from country to country (in Great Britain it rose at an average rate of $3\frac{1}{2}$ per cent per year between 1948 and 1970, whereas in Germany the rate only averaged $2\frac{1}{2}$ per cent), no country has maintained its prices at a constant level. (Note that these are the rates at which prices have been rising, *compounded* over the period as a whole; of course in recent years *annual* rates of inflation have been much higher.) Annual rates of inflation of more than 10 per cent in the past two or three years have not been uncommon.

One might very well ask why, if at all, these facts are significant. Surely it is the quantity and quality of the goods and ser-

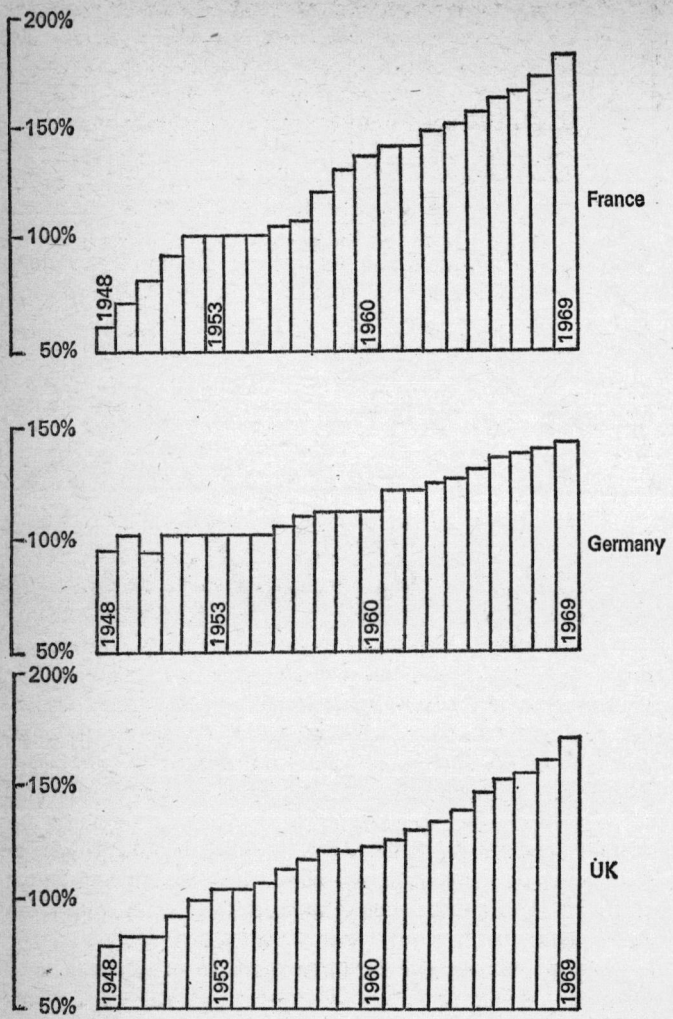

Fig. 1. Price level for consumer goods shown each year as the percentage of its 1953 level

10

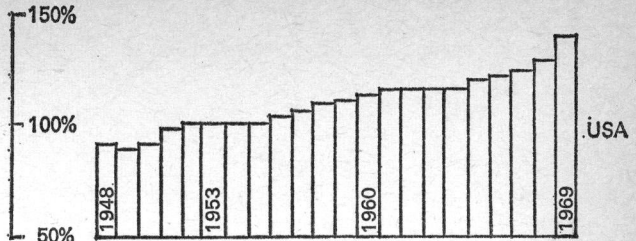

vices that people consume that ultimately determines their standard of living? So long as this is increasing why should the price level matter?

In this and the following sections we hope to give a satisfactory answer to this question. Here we simply hint at some familiar points that will prove useful in developing a full answer.

(I) In periods of rising prices, the prices of different goods and services have not all risen at the same rate. The way consumers and producers have reacted to these differences has affected how much of each gets produced and consumed at any one time.

(II) The fact that prices have not risen uniformly has different effects on the welfare of different sections of the community.

(III) People try to anticipate the rate at which prices will rise in the future. These expectations, and whether they turn out to be right or wrong, influence people's spending and saving habits. This affects the quantity of goods and services produced and the number of people employed.

(IV) Not only have the prices of different goods risen at different rates, but they have risen at different rates in different countries. This has influenced the pattern of world trade and consequently the welfare of the trading countries.

(V) For a variety of reasons, most people maintain sums or 'stocks' of money as part of their wealth, in savings accounts and the like. As prices rise this part of their wealth is reduced and once again their spending and saving patterns may alter.

11

Any rise in prices causes changes in an economy. However, the *rate* at which they have increased seems to be the important issue in the eyes of policy makers, their advisers and their critics. In recent years public figures in many countries have been talking as if the present rate of inflation were unacceptably high. Does this then mean that there is some *acceptable* rate of inflation (inflation is the name we give to a persistent rise in prices) from which we gain more than we lose?

The fact that inflation has persisted for so long may show that it is *not* unacceptable to the authorities. They may feel that a degree of inflation is in some way beneficial to the economy. Or they may not be able to control both inflation and everything else that they want to control, e.g. balance of payments, growth rates, public spending.

For example, it has been thought for some years that full employment is incompatible with stable prices—that *some* unemployment is necessary if prices are to be held down. If the government is acting on this assumption, they will treat the control of inflation and the control of unemployment partly as alternatives. In this context, it is possible that inflation might be considered a 'good thing'. The policy makers have to decide how much inflation is desirable – zero per cent? 5 per cent? 10 per cent?

Whether we think rising prices are undesirable or not, we must know what means governments can use to influence inflation. An understanding of the workings of inflation may help us to assess possible treatments.

## 'PRICE SURVEY RESULTS: MEAT BECOMES DEARER RELATIVE TO OTHER FOODSTUFFS'

We can only begin to assess the efforts of governments to alter or influence price behaviour if we are clear on (i) the role of prices in a modern economy, and (*ii*) the way they are determined.

## WHY DO PRICES MATTER?

Prices have a fundamental influence on the way in which we organise our lives. Imagine what life would be like if you suddenly found yourself required to carry on your everyday business without any knowledge of prices whatsoever.

You must take a job for a month and buy goods and services. Not until the *end* of the month will you be told the various prices of the items you have bought and the wages you have earned. Perhaps you choose the same job as the one you had before your life was rudely interrupted in this way. And perhaps you decide to purchase roughly the same collection of goods and services to which you are accustomed.

Without knowledge of prices and wage rates, it would be coincidental if your receipts in the form of wage earnings just matched your expenditures. Balancing your budget would be a haphazard affair. Possibly some of the goods on your usual shopping list turn out to be very expensive relative to other things that you would not normally purchase. (Potatoes may be extremely expensive and lobsters very cheap.) And perhaps the wage rate for your job is much lower than the one you receive in real life. If you were now permitted to live in this fantasy world with your *new* knowledge of prices and wage rates you could set about reorganising things to the extent of possibly changing your occupation, substituting less expensive goods for more expensive ones and so on.

This little fantasy emphasises the way in which *prices are continually used by us to make allocation decisions*. The following summary picture can be given.

(I) OCCUPATION CHOICE. The wages or salaries attached to various employment opportunities help us to choose between occupations, given our skills and inclinations.

14

(ii) TIME ALLOCATION. We may also use prices to help us decide how to allocate our *time*. The man who forgoes an extra hour of overtime work worth £1 is simultaneously sacrificing an additional £1 worth of goods and services which he might have bought. He does so in order to enjoy an extra hour of leisure. In so doing he is implicitly valuing or pricing his extra hour of leisure at at least £1. Of course if overtime rates were to increase sufficiently, he might work more overtime because an extra hour of leisure would become more and more expensive in terms of the overtime income sacrificed to enjoy it. Its 'price' has increased.

(iii) INCOME ALLOCATION. Income received in whatever form (e.g. for labour services sold or interest payments received on accumulated wealth) is in turn allocated by the consumer. The prices of those goods and services which he might consider buying help him to allocate his income.

We have so far assumed that the consumer has no control over prices. To him they are predetermined. However, while the purchasing decisions of a single consumer will have little or no influence on prices, the combined purchasing decisions of many independent consumers will influence prices through *demand* for goods. We shall examine this mechanism in detail later.

Recent suggestions by government ministers that housewives should 'shop around' in the face of rising food prices are partly based on the idea that combined influence can help to determine the price of goods.

HOW DO PRICES ASSIST US IN MAKING A RATIONAL
ALLOCATION OF OUR INCOME?

We have already seen how prices can help us make the allocation choice between income and leisure. Let us now pursue this allocation process in a little more detail.

The purchase of greater and greater quantities of any one good automatically reduces the possible consumption of other goods. A rational person will limit his purchases of any one good in the following way. He will purchase quantities of it only up to the point where the gain in satisfaction received from a little more of it just balances the consequent loss in satisfaction necessitated by diverting money from the purchase of some other good(s). For instance, let us suppose the price of steak is 80p per pound while that of minced meat is 40p. An

additional pound of steak can be obtained at the expense of two pounds of mince. The relative prices of these goods are in the ratio of two to one. Our description of rational allocation would suggest that the consumer purchase quantities of steak up to the point where the *extra* satisfaction gained from an additional pound of that type of meat be just twice that of an extra pound of mince. If he allocates his income among available goods in this fashion he will reach a position where no further reallocation could increase his total satisfaction from the income available.

These considerations also apply to the way in which we allocate our time between earning income and enjoying leisure.

*Prices therefore, together with income, show us the limits on our choice and guide us to a 'best' (or optimal) allocation.*

Consider a situation in which our consumer has made all his choices of how much of the various goods and services to purchase. He has based this on the knowledge of his available income, the price of each good relative to other prices, and the satisfaction that he feels an additional amount of each good will give him. These are the three ingredients of his choice problem.

A rise in the price of one of these goods (let it be steak for the sake of argument) is announced, all other prices remaining the same. What are the possibilities open to him? Clearly he can no longer buy the same quantity of goods as before, if his income (in money) is fixed.

If he maintains his steak purchases as if nothing had happened, his increased outgoings on steak leave a smaller sum of money available for expenditure elsewhere. In this important aspect the consumer's purchasing possibilities, or *real income,* are reduced by a price rise.

When the price of one good rises relative to that of substitute commodities (steak rises to 90p per pound while mince remains at 40p), it has become more expensive relative to the extra satisfaction that an additional pound of it is bringing him, and more expensive in terms of the amount of mince that has to be given up to enjoy that extra pound of steak.

There will therefore be a *tendency* for the consumer to substitute the *relatively cheaper* good for the one which has become *relatively dearer.*

Clearly, he is worse off after the price change, for while the income he receives in money terms has not changed, his *real*

17

*income,* the overall quantity of goods and services he is able to purchase with his money income, has diminished.

His reaction to the price change will reflect these two facts of (I) *changing relative prices* and (II) *reduced real income.* While the first of these discourages his purchases of steak, whose price has risen, the second may either tend to increase or decrease steak purchases. As a result of the price change he may:

(I) buy the same amount of other goods as before and less steak (amounting to the same *expenditure* as before the price rise);

(II) buy less steak and more mince and the same amount of other things (keeping his meat bill constant);

(III) buy less steak and less mince (reducing his meat bill and reallocating his income elsewhere);

(IV) buy the same amount of steak as before and less of other goods (an increased expenditure on steak);

or more unusually

(V) buy more steak and less of other goods.

Actually this last reaction is unlikely in the case of steak. We include it because there are cases where a price rise has induced an *increase* in the consumption of that good. A more likely situation for this to come about would be where families' diets are largely based on such foods as, say, potatoes, supplemented by a little meat. If the price of *potatoes* rises then quite conceivably the family feels too poor to have as much meat as before. They cut back on meat to sustain the basic intake of potatoes.

*To sum up:* When a single item's price increases, we react to the *specific* effect of the increase in the price of that good relative to others. This reaction on its own would lead us to buy less of that good, and often this is what happens. But the more general, *income* effect of this price rise makes us poorer in real terms.

18

Because we now have to buy less of at least one good, we have to reshuffle the contents of our shopping list. This 'income effect' – so called because it translates a price rise into reduced purchasing possibilities, or reduced real income – may reinforce or counteract the *specific* tendency to buy less of the good whose price has risen. It will depend on the nature of the good in question. You will be able to convince yourself that price rises do not *necessarily* result in reduced consumption of the good in question, by considering what *your* response would be to an increase in housing costs, if all other prices were stable. You do not *necessarily* choose less housing (by moving into poorer quality dwellings). You might well have a shorter holiday instead. In such a case the price rise effect has fallen on 'goods' other than housing.

Much of the time we will conduct our discussion on the assumption that price rises *do* decrease consumption of the good in question, but it is well to bear in mind that there are important exceptions.

*In any case, expenditure patterns will typically change with a change in relative prices, reflecting the fact that some goods become dearer in terms of others and that real incomes alter.*

WHAT WOULD BE THE IMPACT OF A GENERAL PRICE RISE?

So far we have concentrated on two issues, namely: (1) the part which relative prices play in assisting consumers to make allocative choices; (II) readjustments in the pattern of spending which can result from the change in a single price. Let us now examine the possibilities resulting from a *general* rise in prices. Suppose that there occurs an overnight 10 per cent increase in all prices, wages, salaries, rates of interest and so on. What changes might we predict in people's allocations?

At first glance it might seem that so long as this increase is a once-and-for-all change and is not something likely to be repeated, then nothing of substance will change. While all goods and services cost 10 per cent more it is also the case that everyone's income has increased by a corresponding amount. Why then should any readjustment occur?

Unfortunately a consideration of income, prices and people's tastes is not the end of the spending story. For a variety of reasons people do not make all their immediate purchases out of the income they currently receive. At any particular time they will be holding a *sum or 'stock' of money* in the form of cash, or as a chequing account with a bank. Now *any overall price rise is equivalent to a corresponding fall in the purchasing*

*power of money*. So although people's *earnings* have increased by 10 per cent in our example, *part* of their wealth has been eroded through the fall in the value of their money holdings. (At the same time, of course, other components of their wealth such as shares, house property, etc., will have increased in value.) Spenders use part of their money stock to make payments falling due and then replenish this money stock out of their earnings. But now this money stock is worth less from the point of view of its purchasing power. If individuals were holding what they thought to be satisfactory money stocks *before* the price rise they will not be in this happy position after it occurs.

*On the other hand, the rise in the price level reduces the real value of any debts that people have fixed in money terms.* The debtors are now relatively better off than they were before the price rise, and the creditors are relatively worse off. Some readjustment is called for.

HOW MIGHT PEOPLE REACT TO THE CHANGE IN THE PURCHASING POWER OF THEIR MONEY?

(I) *Wage-earners might press for higher payments to compensate for the effect on this part of their wealth.* But since the economy does not consist entirely of wage earners but also of groups which *pay* those wages, we can expect further repercussions from such an attempt.

(II) *Feeling that the real value of their money holdings is now inadequate people might seek to restore it by increasing their saving out of present earnings.* That is to say they would reduce their consumption. Such behaviour, if widespread, would reduce total spending in the economy.

(III) *Alternatively they may try to rebalance their wealth holdings by selling some of their assets which have increased in value* thereby, for example, converting them into cash and restoring the *real* value of their money holdings.

21

To better understand these implications, and the rather different consequences of price rises which are continuing rather than once-and-for-all, we must investigate prices themselves in more detail.

# 2

# 'FIVE LEADING MANUFACTURERS ANNOUNCE PRICE INCREASES'

HOW DO THE PRICES OF INDIVIDUAL PRODUCTS GET DETERMINED?

So far we have treated prices in the way that a single consumer might see them, that is as phenomena over which he has no control but to which he simply responds. Nevertheless, it is important to realise that while the impact of our *individual* purchasing decisions may be imperceptible, when added together over the whole community they actually help to *determine* price. Once again let us begin by referring to a single product. How might the producer of 'Whitewash' soap powder decide on its price?

Products like soap powder are produced by a small number of very large firms. By virtue of their size these firms are able to decide the price at which their product will sell (in contrast to the example of the market gardener given below). What will determine the price at which the producer of 'Whitewash' releases his product to the market?

The price listed on 'Whitewash' will enter the purchasing calculations of housewives. They compare that price per packet with prices of substitute commodities and their subsequent purchase decisions register as *sales*. The number of packets sold, times the price per packet, make up the *revenue* to the producers. A lowering of the price may well result in an increase in sales (if competitors don't decide to match the reduction). But *revenue* (price × quantity sold) may either increase, decrease or remain unchanged! Can you see why this is so?

Take another example, of a greengrocer who has been selling sixty oranges per day at 3p each. His total daily revenue from oranges is 180p. If he lowers the price to 2p and still only manages to sell sixty, his revenue falls to 120p. However, he might sell ninety (total revenue 180p) or 100 (total revenue 200p). On the other hand, he might increase the amount he sells but still have a drop in revenue. This happens if he sells seventy at 2p (total revenue 140p).

The amount by which his sales, and therefore his revenue, will change as a result of his price reduction will depend on how *sensitive* the purchaser's decisions are to price.

The quantity demanded of most products is sensitive in some degree to the price at which they are offered. There will be a possible level of sales corresponding to each possible price and thus a level of revenue (prices × sales). Sales correspond to our notion of demand for a product. These ideas are perhaps most easily seen graphically, as shown in Figure 2 (p. 30).

To return to Whitewash Enterprises. Every packet that they sell has to be produced and the producers thus incur *costs*. The producers' choice of price reaps a revenue from the sales made at that price but also imposes on them the cost of producing that number of packets for sale. Typically, the larger the number of sales, the higher will be those total costs. The relationship between revenue and costs is vital to the producers, the difference representing the level of profits at any chosen price.

If it is the manufacturers' intention to earn the maximum level of profits possible, then they will charge a price which brings about a level of sales that maximises the resulting difference between revenue and costs.

Suppose that Whitewash Enterprises, on considering their potential costs and revenue, decide they can maximise profits by charging 10p per packet. At this price, sales are estimated at 1 million packets per week. When they take all overheads and production costs into consideration, they can produce a very wide range of output quantities at a cost of 8p per packet. This is called the *average cost*. (For very small production levels the average costs would be much higher. This is because the *fixed costs* such as land, administration and other overheads, tend to be similar for many output levels, and are thus a much larger proportion of total costs in the production of small quantities.)

Whitewash Enterprises' weekly accounts show:

| Price | Sales | Total revenue | Total costs | Profit |
|---|---|---|---|---|
| 10p | 1,000,000 | 10p × 1,000,000 | 8p × 1,000,000 | (Revenue minus cost) |
| | | = £100,000 | = £80,000 | £20,000, the best that can be achieved |

Whitewash's marketing people considered other prices before reaching this decision but their calculations showed, for instance:

| Price | Sales | Total revenue | Total costs | Profit |
|---|---|---|---|---|
| 9p | 1,200,000 | 9p × 1,200,000 = £108,000 | 8p × 1,200,000 = £96,000 | £12,000 |
| 11p | 600,000 | 11p × 600,000 = £66,000 | 8p × 600,000 = £48,000 | £18,000 |

That is, by depressing price below 10p sales and revenue increase, but so do costs, in such a way that profits are reduced.

In the example profits fall from £20,000 to £12,000. An increase in price to 11p depresses sales and revenue, but the *lower sales mean lower total costs*. However the *difference* between revenue and costs (i.e. profit) is reduced to £18,000.

In searching for the profit maximising price, it pays the manufacturer to continually reduce price as long as sales and *revenue* are increasing as a result by more than costs. Each additional sale achieved in this way is adding to total profits. When the stage is reached where any *further* price reduction would only add as much to revenue as it would induce in increased costs, it does not pay to reduce price further. The profit maximising price has been found. *Price has been determined by the producer's efforts to maximise profits, while satisfying the demand for the product.*

Suppose that for some reason the demand for Whitewash soap powder increases. Perhaps a consumer association has found it to have a less harmful effect on the skin than its major rival. Or perhaps a competitor has failed and closed down.

This now means that, at any price Whitewash Enterprises decide to charge, they can sell more than they could previously at that price. Before this increase in demand, 10p per packet was the profit maximising price. The increase in demand convinces the producers that if they retain a price of 10p they could sell 1,500,000 packets per week rather than 1,000,000. This would yield an *increase* in profits of £10,000, as the new accounts show.

| Price | Sales | Revenue | Costs | Profit |
|-------|-------|---------|-------|--------|
| 10p | 1,500,000 | 10p × 1,500,000 = £150,000 | 8p × 1,500,000 = £120,000 | £30,000 |

However, the market research team suggest that if they raised the price to 12p, they could *still* maintain *present* sales of 1,000,000, giving

| Price | Sales | Revenue | Costs | Profit |
|-------|-------|---------|-------|--------|
| 12p | 1,000,000 | 12p × 1,000,000 = £120,000 | 8p × 1,000,000 = £80,000 | £40,000 |

26

Even this may not be the *best* Whitewash Enterprises can do in terms of increasing their profit by raising price, but *some* increase in price is obviously to their advantage. They would only be induced to *lower* price if a reduction in average cost per packet could be achieved at the new higher sales level which the lower price would make feasible.

To aid clarity in the example, we have imagined that the cost of producing a packet of 'Whitewash' is independent of the *number* of packets produced. In reality, the producers might be able to make important 'savings' in terms of cost per packet if they increase the level of operation. For example, more highly mechanised plant design, only available for large scale production, might reduce costs. If this were the case, could we still predict that a shift of demand in favour of 'Whitewash' would lead to a rise in price?

Clearly reductions in the *average costs* brought by increasing the level of output would now lead to a different 'best' price. We cannot rule out the case of a price *reduction* being the best strategy for increasing profitability – one example of this occurring is the case of colour television sets.

Probably the most familiar example of a price change that we encounter is that of price increases 'explained' by cost increases. Assume there is no increase in demand. Next assume that 'Whitewash Enterprises' costs rise to 9p per packet, perhaps because the prices of cardboard and chemicals (factors of production) have increased. By maintaining the price of 10p the weekly accounts would now be:

| Price | Sales | Revenue | Costs | Profit |
|---|---|---|---|---|
| 10p | 1,000,000 | £100,000 | 9p × 1,000,000 = £90,000 | £10,000 |

Profits have been halved. Market researchers advise that by raising the product price to 11p Whitewash's sales would fall to 600,000 packets weekly. However *total* costs would be correspondingly reduced, since 400,000 fewer packets would be produced.

| Price | Sales | Revenue | Costs | Profit |
|---|---|---|---|---|
| 11p | 600,000 | 11p × 600,000 = £66,000 | 9p × 600,000 = £54,000 | £12,000 |

The manufacturer can clearly do better by raising price than by not doing so, and there will be some new higher price at which profits are maximised.

*Shifts in the level of demand and changes in the costs of production both contribute to decisions to change price.* These

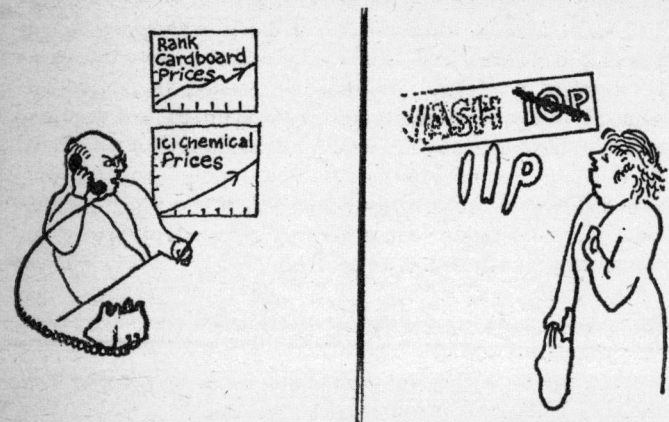

changes should not be confused with the fact that a price, when chosen by the producer, helps to determine the quantity demanded of a good. (It influences the allocation decisions of prospective buyers, remember!)

ARE ALL PRICES ULTIMATELY CHOSEN BY PRODUCERS?

Not all market situations give the scope to a producer that we have just described. In cases where a producer is one of very many offering virtually the same good for sale he may quite correctly view the ruling price as something beyond his control. The individual market-gardener sees the current price for tomatoes at Covent Garden as a price at which he can dispose of whatever he offers. But as a single producer he is not in a position to *quote* a separate price for his tomatoes. Nor will what he *alone* offers for sale, at that price, influence the going price. His contribution to the supply of tomatoes is simply too small to have an impact. He forms an estimate of what the market price will be and, given the revenue and costs that he feels would accompany various output levels, grows that quantity which will maximise profits. He knows he could dispose of whatever he grows at the market price.

If, however, he were to sell part of his produce at a roadside stall he could once more regain some control over the selling price of that part of his output. The product sold in this way becomes distinct from other tomatoes because of the *place* at which it is sold. The quantity demanded at the price quoted at the roadside stall will, nevertheless, reflect the influence of the price of tomatoes elsewhere.

*Producers can act as price-setters or price-takers depending on the nature of the product which they sell, where they choose to sell it and what proportion of the market for it they control.*

(We should mention that, in the case of some nationalised industries, for instance, questions of public welfare will override profit maximisation. Where profits are not the primary consideration, pricing and output decisions will differ from those of the profit maximiser.)

From this point on, we must bear in mind the following relationships:

(I) A consumer's demand for a product reflects the influence of that product's price relative to prices of other goods. It also reflects the additional satisfaction to be had from more of it rather than more of something else.

(II) When these demands are collected over the whole economy they determine the *revenue* to be had by the producers of that product. This revenue, when allied with the cost of production, will influence the price at which the product sells, since it is profit (revenue minus cost) considerations that determine price.

So prices both determine consumers' behaviour and get determined by it! And in this way also it can be seen that the *relative* prices of different goods reflect their *relative* scarcity – 'relative' in the sense of the extra satisfaction that a little more of each would afford the consumer when he has to give up some alternative.

OUR EXAMPLES HAVE SUGGESTED THAT PRICE RISES SHOULD NORMALLY REDUCE THE QUANTITY DEMANDED FOR A PRODUCT WHILE PRICE REDUCTIONS SHOULD STIMULATE IT. WHY THEN DO WE SO OFTEN OBSERVE IN REAL LIFE COMPANIES' SALES EXPAND-ING EVEN THOUGH THEY ARE RAISING PRICES?

This seeming inconsistency is quickly disposed of when we realise that prices of products are not the only things that change. To concentrate attention on the '*pure*' influence of prices on quantities demanded, we have pushed other influences into the background. For example, at the same time as a consumer is reappraising his or her purchases of tomatoes

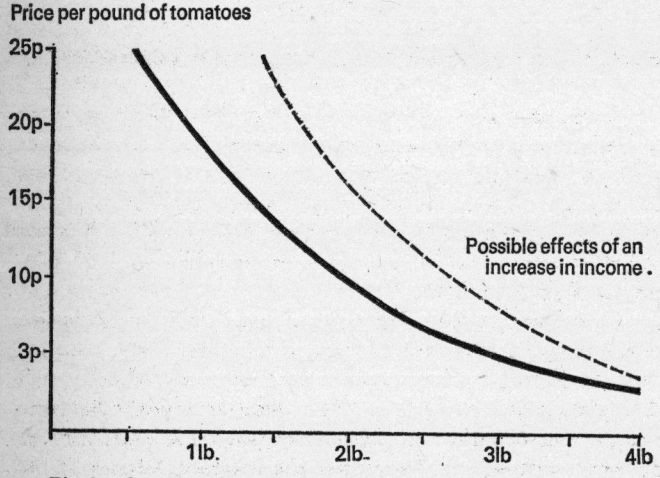

Fig. 2. Quantity of tomatoes purchased each week by household

because of their increased relative price, a rise in consumer *income* might occur, so that it is possible to buy more of everything including tomatoes. What our theory really says can be put in one of two ways:

(I) *The 'higher the price the lower the quantity demanded' idea is one which treats other factors as if they remain unchanged. In reality income increases may well increase quantities demanded at* EVERY *price.*

(II) *Even if incomes do increase we will buy less of the good* THAN OTHERWISE *if its price rises.*

# 'COTTON-SPINNING INDUSTRY INSTALLS FURTHER LABOUR-SAVING EQUIPMENT TO COUNTER INCREASED LABOUR COSTS'

HOW DO PRICE CHANGES AFFECT PRODUCTION TECHNIQUES?

So far we have largely directed our enquiry at the question of the prices charged for goods and services. But business firms are also preoccupied with other sets of prices – those of the *factors of production (inputs)*, men, equipment and raw materials – that make output possible. Input (or factor) prices influence costs and dictate the most efficient way of producing a *chosen* output.

To say that business enterprises endeavour to maximise profits is also to say that they try to minimise costs – to produce the desired level of output in the least costly way. *The fact that it is possible, to some extent at least, to produce the same output level by different means, using different combinations of men, machines and raw materials, generates interest in the prices of the factors of production.*

31

The difference between agricultural techniques used to grow corn in India and the United States is due not only to the state of agricultural technology in those countries but also to the availability of the factors used. Machinery is cheap relative to labour in the United States, and expensive relative to labour in India. Hence 'labour-intensive' methods are more efficient, in an economic sense, in India, and 'capital-intensive' methods are more appropriate to the United States.

In much the same way as consumers respond to changes in the relative prices of the goods they purchase, business management responds to changes in the relative prices of the productive factors it uses. If the hire of labour becomes more expensive relative to machinery, we can expect a tendency for machines to be substituted for manpower. To what extent this is possible and profitable depends partly on the technology of particular industries. For instance an airline confronted by rising costs of flight crews might decide to replace ten of its existing aircraft with five Jumbo jets. Jumbos, however, require *larger* flight crews and more service staff and the airline may not wish to seriously reduce the number of flights offered to customers. The extent of the substitution of capital equipment for labour will be tempered by these considerations. Nevertheless some degree of substitution is usually open to firms.

*Changes in input prices influence the combination in which firms use those inputs as they try to produce each item at the lowest possible cost.*

ARE THERE ANY CASES IN WHICH CHANGES IN THE RELATIVE PRICES OF INPUTS, SUCH AS A WAGE RISE WHICH RAISES THE

RELATIVE PRICE OF LABOUR, WILL NOT LEAD TO SUBSTITUTION
OF OTHER FACTORS?

*The extent to which wages rises will lead to the substitution of other factors for labour will depend on labour's contribution to the product in question. If this contribution (productivity) rises sufficiently in the face of rising wages then it is possible that no substitution of alternative inputs will occur.*

# 3

# 'LEADING MANUFACTURER: "EXCESSIVE WAGE SETTLEMENTS HAVE FORCED REDUNDANCY"'

### HOW ARE WAGE RATES AND EMPLOYMENT RELATED?

We generally understand by inflation a situation in which both money prices and money wages are increasing. In recent years inflation has also been accompanied by unemployment in the British economy. If we wish to understand something of the relationship between all three features, we must first discover how wages get determined. By 'getting determined' we mean not so much the actual bargaining processes between unions and management, crucial though they may be. Rather we wish to focus on the underlying forces that are influencing these two groups and affecting the likely outcome of any negotiations. We concentrate on the things that place limits on possible results of bargaining.

*We must examine the forces that influence the supply of labour and the demand for it.*

### DOES THE DEMAND FOR LABOUR RESEMBLE THE DEMAND FOR GOODS?

Goods are demanded because they yield satisfaction to those who consume them. The fact that they are costly necessitates *choice* among them. We have described the balancing process made, perhaps unconsciously, by a consumer in adjusting the extra satisfaction from more consumption of a particular good to the extra expenditure entailed. Moreover we have seen how a fall or rise in the price of a good relative to other prices may increase or decrease the quantity of it which is demanded.

Now the factors of production – labour, capital equipment, industrial land, etc., don't yield satisfaction directly to the firms that employ them. What they do yield is *output* and sale of that output brings *revenue*. Also, their use entails *costs*.

Revenues and costs are the two ingredients of profits. It seems natural to conclude that if firms are interested in maximising profits, they will demand additional quantities of an input only so long as those quantities are making at least as big an addition to revenue as they are to costs.

*In this 'balancing-process' sense the demand for productive factors, including labour, resembles the demand for a good.*

HOW DOES LABOUR'S PRODUCTIVITY LIMIT ITS USE?

To spotlight the role of productivity alone we will sacrifice some realism by supposing, temporarily, that only *labour* inputs can be altered.

One of the most important observations of early students of economic systems was that, as a producer combines more and more labour with a *fixed* amount of other productive factors, the additions to output that he can achieve in this way will *eventually* begin to fall off. We illustrate with an example. The following schedule shows what Whitewash could expect in the way of additional (or marginal) output if they step up labour use, keeping the amount of other inputs, e.g. machinery, fixed.

| Man-hours used | Total production (packets) | Additional (marginal) product from an extra man hour |
|---|---|---|
| 100 | 1,000 | 10 |
| 101 | 1,010 | 12 |
| 102 | 1,022 | 8 |
| 103 | 1,030 | 5 |
| 104 | 1,035 | 4 |
| 105 | 1,039 | |

Now suppose this extra output is sold by the producer at a price of 10p per packet. Then corresponding to the additional or 'marginal' product schedule there is a 'marginal revenue product' schedule – the additional output from an extra man-hour multiplied by the money value of that output (see Figure 3).

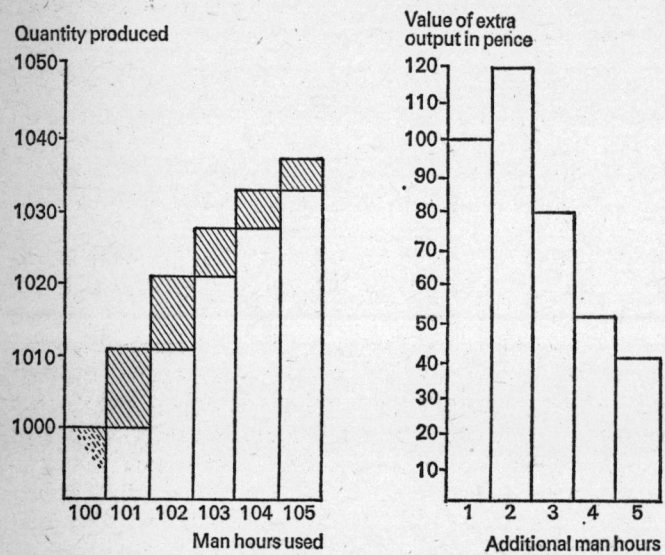

Fig. 3. Declining marginal productivity (shaded area)

Imagine that an additional hour of labour costs 50p to purchase. That is to say, 50p is the hourly wage rate, no matter whether the producer is hiring 100 or 103 or 130 hours of labour. Under these circumstances, he will stop hiring additional labour after 104 hours is reached. At that point he earns an additional 50p in revenue from the last hour hired but also incurs 50p in additional wage costs. Up to this point he is better than breaking even. This is the point of balance we have referred to. (Compare it with the consumer's problem of balancing his expenditures!)

*At a fixed wage rate and price for the final product, the employment of labour by a firm will be limited to the point where additional costs of a further unit of labour just equal the additional revenue obtainable from the extra output of that unit of labour.*

It is a simple matter to establish the effects of an increase in labour's productivity. If you rework the example supposing the following schedule,

| Man-hours used | Total production | Marginal product |
| --- | --- | --- |
| 100 | 1,010 | 12 |
| 101 | 1,022 | ? |
| 102 | 1,036 | ? |
| 103 | 1,046 | ? |
| 104 | 1,058 | ? |
| 105 | 1,063 | |

with the same hourly wage rate and price of the finished article, the new point of balance is reached at 105 man-hours rather than at 104.

*When labour becomes more productive it becomes cheaper in one sense because a higher output can be obtained for the same outlay as before.* When this happens, as long as it is not necessary to reduce price substantially to dispose of the extra product, it will be profitable to expand production and use more labour. If there is an increase in productivity of the type shown in the example, but it is necessary to drop the price of the finished article to 8p per packet in order to dispose of the total production of 105 man hours, then the additional revenue obtained by hiring 105 rather than 104 is only $8p \times (1,063 - 1,058) = 40p$, whereas the additional cost is 50p. Clearly increased labour use to this level is not profitable.

HOW DOES THE DEMAND FOR THE FINAL PRODUCT AFFECT THE DEMAND FOR LABOUR?

In contrast to the last example, suppose there is an increase in the demand for the finished product such that the firm can now sell all it can produce using 105 man-hours (or any smaller total) at a new price of 12½p. With the wage rate still at 50p it would now be profitable to extend labour use to 105 man-hours. This is why: using our first example (p. 35), at the new price of 12½p, 104 man-hours rather than 103 means an increase in revenue of $(5 \times 12\frac{1}{2}) = 62\frac{1}{2}$p, while the cost of the additional hour of labour is only 50p. Only by increasing labour use by a *further* hour to 105 will the increase in revenue $(4 \times 12\frac{1}{2}$p = 50p) be *just* offset by the additional cost, 50p.

*Increases in the demand for the final product, like increases in labour productivity, increase the whole schedule of marginal revenues obtainable from labour. As a result more of that factor will be employed at the ruling wage rate.*

HOW DOES THE WAGE RATE AFFECT THE QUANTITY OF LABOUR DEMANDED?

Given the original price of 10p per packet and the original marginal productivity schedule, we leave it to you to calculate the impact of an increase in the hourly wage from 50p to 80p. It is now inadvisable to hire labour beyond 103 hours.

The picture on the demand for labour can be summarised as follows:

*It may be expected that the demand for labour varies according to the conditions under which labour can be obtained (the wage rate), what can be done with it once it is obtained (its marginal productivity), and what can be done with this product (demand for the final good).*

Where the demand for the final product does not change, the demand for labour is a relationship between its marginal revenue product and the wage rate.

The previous examples demonstrate this point. But in supporting this conclusion we have passed over the role of *other* inputs and their prices. To highlight the relation between labour productivity and wages, we assumed that our manufacturer was not able to vary the amount of other inputs. As we have hinted before, when the price of labour increases, there may be some opportunity to substitute other inputs for it and there will be an inducement to do that if their prices have not changed. For example, if the wages of clerks rise relative to the price of computers (which can do the same job), a producer might well consider it worth his while to sack the clerks and hire a computer.

So we must amend our view of influences on the demand for labour and include the prices of other inputs and the ease of substituting these inputs for labour. We are only justified in ignoring them in situations where these cannot be varied (e.g. when capital equipment is being used to capacity and cannot be readily added to).

HOW DO WAGES AND PRICES TOGETHER INFLUENCE THE QUANTITY OF LABOUR DEMANDED?

Where other conditions remain unchanged, employers will demand more labour if money wages fall. This lower money wage offsets the drop in marginal productivity of the extra labour. Producers will also increase employment if they can dispose of *present* output levels at a *higher* price. (Note: when did any money wages last fall?)

Wage increases and price increases push in opposite directions on the quantity of labour demanded. Price rises tend to increase it when they are symptoms of an increased demand for the things that labour produces. Increases in money wages depress it. These two effects can be considered together in what is called the *real wage*.

$$\text{Real wage} = \frac{\text{Money wage}}{\text{Price level}}$$

The real wage might rise as a result of rising money wage levels and a constant or falling price level. It might rise because both money wages and prices rise but the money wage undergoes the bigger increase. Looking at the effects of money wages, and then the effects of prices, on employers' demands for labour, we can deduce that *the quantity of labour de-*

*manded by employers is* REDUCED *by* INCREASES *in the real wage and* INCREASED *by* FALLS *in the real wage.*

## WHAT DETERMINES THE SUPPLY OF LABOUR?

Moving from the employers' point of view to the people actually offering their labour for hire, we would again expect real wages to be significant. Now the effects are reversed. A higher real wage rate (money wages adjusted for the price level) would, as we have argued earlier, make leisure relatively more expensive. Currently employed people might be expected to offer themselves for more overtime. Housewives may be tempted back into the labour market by these higher real wages and so on. *We would expect that the quantity of labour supplied is increased by increases in the real wage and decreased by falls in it.* (However, there are signs that some people establish a 'target income' level. They want to earn, say, £3,000 per year and are satisfied once they have achieved that level. In that case, despite the fact that a rise in real wages raises the relative price of leisure, they may opt to maintain their income level and work shorter hours when wage rates rise.)

## WHEN IS THE LABOUR MARKET IN BALANCE?

*The labour market is in balance when the amount of work being offered by employers (the quantity of labour demanded) is equal to the quantity supplied by workers.* But both quantities demanded and supplied are responses to the real wage and we can think of a real wage level being established that just balances the two sides. At a lower real wage, demand would tend to exceed supply and at a higher one supply would dominate. Either of these conditions would create pressures on the prevailing real wage to drive it back towards the position of balance. *So movements in real wages should tend to balance labour supply and demand, or so this mechanism would suggest.*

WHY ISN'T BALANCE AUTOMATIC, AND WHY DOES BRITAIN
EXPERIENCE UNEMPLOYMENT LEVELS OF OVER 800,000?

We have built up a picture of the demand for and supply of
labour in the economy as a whole as though it were a simple
collection of plans and responses of individual employers and
employees.

If the real wage is the 'price' which equates labour demand
with labour supply, and if there are 800,000 people unemployed (seeking to supply their labour) and only 400,000 job
vacancies, why don't real wages fall to eliminate this excess
supply? In shifting the emphasis from a single producer or
wage-earner to the economy as a whole, *we have glossed over
several important issues which must now be incorporated to
give a true picture.*

We first examine the jump from employment questions at the level of the individual firm to those at the economy-wide level. We must consider the interdependence among the millions of decision-takers who constitute 'the economy'. This interdependence can make arguing from the particular case to the general a tricky business.

Furthermore, we have supposed the possibility of balance between labour supply and demand to rest on the ability of the real wage to adjust to the pressures of supply and demand. We have assumed that prices or money wages or both will move in the appropriate direction to restore balance in the labour market. Could it be that the adjustment of either or both of these components of the real wage is faulty or inhibited in some way ... that they fail to respond to a situation where labour supply exceeds demand? *Perhaps prices fail to rise adequately because of the depressed level of demand for the final product, so producers are not enticed into profitably expanding production. Or perhaps money wages are artificially maintained at too high a level for unemployment to eliminate itself automatically.*

## WHAT PREVENTS MONEY WAGES FROM FALLING WHEN UNEMPLOYMENT EXISTS?

It might be very tempting to answer 'The Unions'! Indeed there would be some truth in this. But it would still remain for us to answer why the unions, striving, presumably, for workers' welfare, should not adjust their wage demands to the plight of some of their members. Why not modify wage requests and reduce unemployment levels?

Such a strategy is unacceptable to unions. Their chief method of redistributing wealth in favour of employees appears to be the increased money wage that they can extract through bargaining. Unions don't for the most part strike wage agreements in real terms. They do so in money terms – so many pounds per week or so many pence per hour. In situations where the aggregate output of the economy is growing (but where nevertheless unemployment exists) workers come to *expect* increases in their real wage – increases in the number of goods they can buy at present prices with their money wage. Money wage rises would seem to be the natural way to fulfil these expectations. Union demands reflect these expectations.

Nor may this action be entirely at odds with the wishes and aspirations of the *unemployed* workers. They too have ideas about what they are worth. A freshly unemployed man does not accept the first job vacancy that comes along at perhaps something less than the wage he has been earning. Much in the way of somebody offering an antique for sale at an auction, he will have a reserve price below which he will not immedi-

ately accept work. Rather he will search for a better prospect. Only after he has endured a series of frustrations in this search, and has perhaps been forced to dip heavily into past savings, may he revise his reserve price downwards.

But at this stage a different snag appears in the balancing process. People register as unemployed. But by and large they do not, nor can they, advertise the fact that they are prepared to work at a lower money wage. For one thing minimum wage agreements inhibit this. So does the fact that there are no general labour 'markets' in which potential employees can declare the price at which they are prepared to offer their skills and where employers can react to such offers.

*Union claims almost invariably take the form of money wage claims (working conditions we will neglect here). These claims reflect expectations about real wages in a growing economy. Since unions don't have the power to lower the prices of goods, they seek to improve their real wage by bidding up money wages. This fact, together with their reluctance, and then inability, to adjust the price at which they can sell their skills, can stop money wages from falling even in the face of quite severe unemployment.*

MONEY WAGES DID FALL DURING THE 'GREAT DEPRESSION' OF THE THIRTIES BUT UNEMPLOYMENT PERSISTED. WHY?

A trite answer suggests itself. Money wages did not fall far enough, since goods' prices were also falling. *Real* wages therefore remained at a level which was too high to equate labour supply and demand. But the answer is not this simple – economic answers seldom are, as the reader is probably beginning to suspect. The following subsidiary questions might be examined.

(I) Were real wage levels at the onset of the Depression really too high or were they right for full employment and was something else wrong?

(II) Even if real wages were wrong for full employment and got further out of alignment as the depression got deeper because of the failure of wages to fall as fast as prices, would a policy of money wage reduction have restored full employment? Or does the economy lack the automatic balancing mechanisms that we suggested exist, in theory, for equating supply and demand for labour?

We trace out the likely behaviour of an economy lapsing

into recession (a state characterised by widespread unemployment) in order to shed light on these problems. We are close to important theories of the way recessions develop if we suppose that initially businessmen change their expectations about the future. They revise their expectations about demand for their product. They may have been predicting steady increases in the demand for their product (increasing sales at the prevailing level of prices), predictions which they now have reason to change. Consequently they may reduce the stock holdings on their shelves and cut orders for capital equipment intended for output expansion. Such order reductions will be felt as an excess supply developing in the industries that produce these capital or 'investment' goods. These industries are experiencing an *actual reduction in demand* as opposed to merely a revision in expectations. A smaller output of investment goods seems called for on the grounds of profitability, men are laid off in the investment goods industries and a recession has begun.

Unless the employees in these industries producing machine tools, primary metal products, buildings, building materials and the like, could have anticipated the reduction in orders with the immediate acceptance of reduced money wages which might ensure their continued employment, there is little reason to expect that this first round of deflation could have been avoided. But the *information flows* in our economy are not that perfect. Even if they were, could we reasonably expect building workers, furnacemen, sheet metal workers and lathe makers to rationalise such a move? They might reasonably be expected to ask:

'Why should we be the buffers against recession? Our employers, the manufacturers of goods for capital expansion, have experienced a reduction in demand. They can no longer sell the present quantity of output at prevailing prices. The demand price has fallen. But why should we suffer relative to other trades by being guaranteed full employment only at the expense of reduced wages? It is the responsibility of the authorities to intervene in the economy to raise the demand price for these goods and so stabilise employment.'

45

*But among economists there are a great number who believe that even if such wage reductions were feasible, rather than innoculating the economic system against further unemployment, they would actually be encouraging it!*

WHY MIGHT WAGE REDUCTIONS AGGRAVATE RECESSION INSTEAD OF HELPING TO RELIEVE IT?

Let us summarise the situation facing an economy on the verge of decline into depression. Producers of final goods for consumption by the spending public have revised their expectations about sales.

They reduce orders for new capital equipment. There is now an excess supply of these investment goods.

Lay-offs occur in these industries and, we suppose, wage reductions eventually become possible.

One line of reasoning would suggest that this fall in the real wage in the investment goods industries should make it possible to restore employment in these industries to its former levels. But how can this be? It means restoring output to its old level. And the people making consumer goods don't want all this output. Are they tempted to restore orders for new capital equipment because it has become relatively cheaper (its price has fallen)? This would not help employment matters overall if it simply means that consumer goods manufacturers adhere to reduced output plans using relatively more capital equipment than before. For this would entail sackings of workers making consumer goods.

'Why then', proclaims the optimist, 'with a little goodwill on the part of workers in the consumer goods industries their wages could be reduced, thereby enabling the prices of finished goods to come down and the sales of these consumer goods to expand. After all, it seemed to be the anticipated reductions in consumer goods sales that started the trouble in the first place.'

But it is at this point that the sceptics step in, if they have not done so already. Far from helping to restore the consumer goods industries to health, they insist, those wage reductions

46

already put into effect will be helping to make the original dismal prophecies of consumer goods manufacturers self-fulfilling. Reduced money wages have meant smaller money income for those receiving them and it is largely upon these incomes that their spending depends. At the same time as investment goods industries are trying to signal to consumer goods manufacturers the attractiveness of their new lower prices, those very same consumer goods manufacturers are feeling the reduced spending of the now lower-paid workers in the investment goods industries and of those already out of work.

As an example, suppose that women decide to buy fewer dresses (perhaps because the price of food has risen and they allocate a larger share of their real income to food). Then there will be a fall in the demand for sewing machines, and sackings of machinists and machine makers. Now the income of the machinists and machine makers falls, their demand for dresses falls, and so the cycle continues.

*Because wages are incomes and incomes limit spending, reductions in wages will lead to further cut-backs in output and employment as producers experience reduced sales. Here is the interdependence that we spoke of earlier; it is the interdependence of Incomes and Expenditures.*

Ours is an economy in which goods and services are offered in return for money incomes, and money expenditures are made to obtain such goods and services. Goods and services are not swapped directly for other goods and services. Money flows are the impulses which drive our economic machinery. Producers respond to them. Consequently, even if money wages of, say, building workers, fell sufficiently to maintain, temporarily, full employment in the face of reduced construction demand, their reduced money incomes would be felt as reduced expenditure *elsewhere*. Unemployed building workers have less to spend. Retail receipts fall. This would be a signal for contraction elsewhere. So the seeming paradox that reduced labour costs can lead to contraction is resolved.

These considerations lead us naturally to an examination of changes in expenditure at the economy-wide level. But this aggregate expenditure must in some way be linked to demand – to aggregate demand.

# 4

# 'DEMAND REACHES DANGEROUS HIGH'

WHAT IS MEANT BY AN INCREASE IN AGGREGATE DEMAND?

When referring to an individual good or service we have used the term 'demand' to denote the actual quantity of that good or service that people are prepared to buy at various prices. Demand is a relationship between quantities and prices. The 'quantity demanded' refers to the physical amount (bags of coal, hours of tuition or whatever) that people are prepared to buy at the prevailing price. An 'increase in demand' refers to the fact that people are prepared to buy more at each and every price level for that good than before. It also means that they are prepared to pay a higher price than the present one to obtain the same amount of that good. Both interpretations involve the ability to increase total money outlay on that good. This is also true of aggregate demand.

*When we speak of an increase in the demand for goods and services in the aggregate, we are referring to willingness and ability to increase aggregate expenditure on goods and services at the prevailing level of prices.*

WHAT COMPRISES AGGREGATE DEMAND?

For purposes of analysis, it is convenient to break up aggregate demand into several categories. This enables us to recognise the different influences which help to *determine the level* of aggregate demand.

*The demand for consumer goods and services* is the largest single element of aggregate demand. It is the summation of individual spenders' demands. So it will depend on the various factors determining individual demand. These include a sub-jective element, the preference for consumption now rather than later – the idea that the sooner we can enjoy something the better.

But it will also be linked to the ability to make payment

for goods purchased and so will depend on wealth, including money balances held by consumers. Income is the means of replenishing that wealth. Since many consumption purchases are made by exchanging money in hand for goods, economists have focused on income as the main determinant of consumer demand. Income is money in hand, immediately available for spending. Wealth, on the other hand, has to be 'realised' or 'liquidated' before it can be turned into consumption. Shares have to be sold – turned into money – before they can be spent on the purchase of a Spanish holiday.

Investigations, however, have indicated that consumer demand is not so closely tied to current earnings as was previously thought. Borrowing facilities exist. People can mortgage things, can borrow money using assets as security, can even in some circumstances receive loans on the basis of their likely future earning power. *In doing so they weaken the link between present income and present spending that we discussed in the context of spiralling unemployment.*

Borrowing and lending involve a reorganisation of the pattern of consumption through time. In 'bringing forward' consumption, borrowers have to give up some at a future date. Loans must be repaid with interest. We can expect prevailing rates of interest to influence people in making a balanced assessment of their consumption pattern. Some will be deciding to save out of present earnings, to lend their savings at interest and thereby to enlarge future consumption, while others will be borrowing in favour of greater present consumption. *A rise in interest rates makes borrowed consumption dearer and future consumption relatively cheaper.*

We have seen that the relative prices of goods and services influence our allocation of income among those things we are considering purchasing. In an overall sense the present level of prices versus their anticipated future behaviour may affect our overall present demands. The rate at which prices are expected to change can have a bearing on borrowing and lending, on spending and saving, on present versus future demand. This influence is likely to be strongest among what are called *durable* goods. A man who anticipates an acceleration of milk and bread prices is hardly likely to negotiate a loan with his bank to facilitate an 'eat now pay later' food spree. He may however seek to bring forward his purchase of a washing machine or power drill if he anticipates a rise in their prices.

*Investment*, the demand for producer goods – stocks on the shelves and new equipment – is another important component of aggregate demand. It is less directly tied to the incomes received by consumers than is consumption demand, but it is not entirely unrelated to them. Net investment is the addition to the existing stock of capital equipment in the economy. It is closely linked to considerations of profitability. Expanding firms must make estimates of future returns to be had from adding to their capital stock. The owner of a corner shop may be contemplating an extension to his premises to convert to a supermarket.

Before seeking a loan to finance such a venture, he considers the additional future profits to be had from the extension. If he expects them to exceed his loan repayments he may decide to go ahead. Higher and higher rates of interest will make such investment successively less attractive, by making repayments larger. They increase the amount that has to be recovered before the new capital is paying its way. *In this way the level of investment is dependent on interest rates, or perhaps, more precisely, on what interest rates are expected to be in future.* Just how strong this dependence is has been a matter of some controversy among economists. Upon it hangs the effectiveness of attempts to influence the level of aggregate demand by altering the rate of interest (as for example a 'credit squeeze').

Investment demand is not altogether isolated from consumer incomes. It is out of these incomes that purchases are made of goods and services that are produced only through the *use* of capital equipment provided by investment. We have already seen how anticipations about these purchases affect investment and how they can make it quite unstable.

*Government requirements* of various kinds contribute to aggregate demand. Public as well as private consumption must be included in the overall demand for goods and services. The fact that the government rather than an individual purchases the services of a dentist or doctor makes it none the less a demand for medical services. A multitude of other government purchases connected with the civil service, defence, the national road network and so on must be similarly treated. Government demand is distinguished from private demand by the factors that determine the level of this spending and the way in which it is financed.

Such demands, where they can be varied according to government plan, are a part of the machinery available for regulating the economy. Just as fluctuations in private consumer demand can influence employment levels, so can public spending. It is part of the so-called 'fiscal measures' of government budget control. There are elements of government demand which are consumer demand in a public sense – where the government simply takes over the role of spender in satisfying current consumer demands, as in the case of the Health Service. Other elements are in the nature of investment demand. The construction of a new stretch of motorway provides for future consumption of transport services.

Not all demand for domestically produced goods and services originates in Britain. The very important *export sector* reflects foreign demands for British products both of a consumer and capital good nature. Similarly the demand by British buyers for *foreign* goods is not part of aggregate demand for British goods, but registers naturally enough as demand in the countries where those goods are produced.

*Aggregate demand can be thought of as the total consumption and investment demands of both the public and private sectors, together with the demand for exports. It depends on whatever they depend on.*

INVESTMENT IS AN ELEMENT OF AGGREGATE DEMAND. IS IT NOT ALSO AN ELEMENT OF AGGREGATE SUPPLY?

Investment is an addition to the existing stock of capital. Capital, like labour and raw materials, is one of the productive factors from which output is obtained. One might therefore ask: 'Is not an enlargement of the capital stock simultaneously adding to the flow of output – to aggregate supply?' The answer is that *current investment is an alternative to some current consumption as it uses resources that could be devoted to that end. What it does is to enlarge the potential for future aggregate supply*. There is a time-lag between the accumulation of new capital and its contribution to output for consumption.

## DON'T INCREASES IN AGGREGATE DEMAND LEAD AUTOMATICALLY TO INCREASES IN AGGREGATE SUPPLY AND VICE VERSA?

We have already identified with increases in aggregate demand the willingness and ability to increase *expenditure* at the prevailing price level. But we have also pointed out that every expenditure is also a receipt for someone else. When we look at the extra expenditure generated by increased aggregate demand, we can see that it has its exact counterpart in terms of increased incomes received.

*In this strict expenditure and income sense aggregate demand and aggregate supply are always equal. But this is nothing more than an accounting truism.* In the same sense that a businessman's books always balance, so the economy's 'books' relating income and expenditure always balance. Because it is always true this view sheds little light on the way in which things, including prices, *change* in the economy.

## IN WHAT SENSE THEN CAN AGGREGATE DEMAND AND AGGREGATE SUPPLY DIVERGE?

It is worthwhile restating an account of economic processes already encountered in our study of depression situations. Depressions have their counterpart in inflationary states. In dealing with the behaviour of an economic system such as our own, we are faced with the fact that literally millions of decisions about spending and saving, supplying and investing, pricing and offering terms of employment, are being made simultaneously. Individuals, firms and governments make plans (on the basis of expectations) which, when put into effect, will interact with one another, and will be influenced in their working by how past plans are working out at present.

*There is no vast central computer co-ordinating individuals' plans to supply skills, to earn incomes or to purchase goods with the plans of businessmen to demand labour services from them to produce and sell goods.*

Rather, information as to changes in plans or divergence of

events from what was expected filters imperfectly through the system as those plans are put into effect. Firms may find their plans failing to materialise with unexpected accumulation or run down of stocks on their shelves. Shortages or surpluses of labour offering itself for sale may emerge at existing prices. These shortages and surpluses may also mean frustration of *consumers'* plans for current spending.

Just as quantities can diverge from their anticipated levels, confounding various plans as they do so, so can prices. An industry may be confronted with an unexpectedly large pay settlement to deal with. A consumer may have to contend with unanticipated price rises for some goods as firms use price increases, either to ration existing supplies in the face of demand increases, or to try and preserve profits by passing on cost increases. *In the aggregate it is always possible, and indeed most probable, that demands and supplies will diverge in the planned sense. Such divergence produces tendencies for change.*

One of our primary aims is to give the reader a basis for considering the process of inflation. Any study of inflation is intimately concerned with *price* behaviour. But price behaviour is inextricably linked with the behaviour of *quantities* demanded and supplied. *Both* prices and quantities tend to adjust as the result of divergence in supply and demand plans. Inflation is partly a question of how much and how fast these two elements adjust in these divergent or 'disequilibrium' situations.

# 5

# 'PRICES RISE AT 10% PER YEAR WHILE OUTPUT STAGNATES'

UNDER WHAT CIRCUMSTANCES WILL CHANGES IN AGGREGATE
EXPENDITURE (PRICES × QUANTITIES SOLD) BE LARGELY COM-
POSED OF PRICE CHANGES RATHER THAN OUTPUT CHANGES?

Let us suppose that for some reason or other people find themselves in possession of extra spending power. Perhaps the government decides to run a Budget Deficit (to spend more than it receives), and finances its extra spending by having the Bank of England print more money. This cash is used by government departments to make purchases. It finds its way into the hands of the public. Before anything else has had a chance to change, people adjust their demands for goods and services.

As increased orders make themselves known to distributors and producers, two things are likely to happen. First of all, firms find it profitable to raise prices to ration, among purchasers, existing stocks and goods coming off the production line. Even if they wish to do so, there are limits on the extent to which firms can *immediately* increase the quantity supplied under these changed circumstances. For one thing, they are encumbered by the size of their existing stock of capital equipment which cannot be immediately expanded.

In order that any expansion at all be possible it may be necessary to offer higher rates of pay in the form of overtime payments to labour. Offers of higher rates of pay to attract labour away from other industries or out of waiting for more attractive offers may have to be made.

In an industry in which existing capital cannot be used more fully with the same amount of labour, or where insufficient time has elapsed to bring new capital equipment into effect, the only feasible way of enlarging present output may be through hiring extra labour.

We have previously stressed that as more and more labour is brought into the productive process with a fixed amount of capital equipment, the resulting *increases* in output taper off.

*If output can only be expanded at greater and greater cost, higher and higher prices will have to be paid by those demanding the extra output if its production is to be profitable. Under such circumstances price increases should quickly dominate output increases.*

IS IT ONLY IN SITUATIONS OF NEAR-FULL EMPLOYMENT THAT CHANGES IN AGGREGATE EXPENDITURE ARE PRINCIPALLY MADE UP OF PRICE CHANGES RATHER THAN OUTPUT CHANGES?

Available evidence suggests that the answer is 'no.' We have deliberately told the story of *increased money in circulation leading to increased expenditure* in a situation where firms have little excess productive capacity and where there is not a large pool of surplus labour. This introduced the idea of 'full-employment inflation' induced by a change in the money supply. It is not close enough to actual experience to furnish an adequate explanation of the inflationary tendencies we have experienced in recent years.

The price level has continued to rise even in situations where substantial unemployment has existed, when our theory tells us little pressure should be being exerted on prices.

*A theory which suggests that changes in aggregate spending are largely made up of changes in* REAL *output when there is unemployment and largely of* PRICE *increases when the economy is fully employed does not fit with the facts.* It is sad but true that economics cannot at present boast a satisfactory theory that explains consistently the breakdown of aggregate expenditure changes into price movements and real output movements. Let us look further at some of the difficulties surrounding this vexed question.

# 'FAILURE TO CONTROL MONEY SUPPLY HAS BROUGHT INFLATIONARY CONSEQUENCES'

MUST AN INCREASE IN THE MONEY SUPPLY INEVITABLY GENERATE PRICE INCREASES?

If greater numbers of goods and services are produced this year than last, we speak of an increase in real output. If this increased production is sold at the same prices as last year the money value of transactions has also increased. If last year 100 items were exchanged at a price of £1 each and this year an additional 50 are sold, then the money value of transactions has increased by £50. To make this increased exchange possible, either (I) the amount of money – whatever has been used as a means of payment in these transactions – has been increased to cope with the extra volume of trade, or (II) the existing money has had to circulate faster through the economy, doing more exchange 'work' than last year and, as a consequence, is held idle (as cash in hand or as untouched bank deposits) for a shorter period than before.

Alternatively, if the same amount of goods and services are produced as last year but are exchanged at higher prices, once again the money value of transactions has increased. And once again more money in the economy, or faster circulation, is required.

We could take a different approach, analysing the consequences of a change in the supply of money in the economy. If the quantity of money available increases, either (I) the money value of transactions increases, or (II) the speed at which money circulates falls and the effects of the increase in the money supply are cancelled out because people decide to hold on to money for longer periods than previously. (Why they would want to do this is a question to be discussed shortly.) A combination of both effects (III) is of course possible. Included in (III) are the possibilities that prices alone rise or that

58

production alone rises with prices remaining constant; or perhaps a rise in both takes place.

Both prices and quantities of goods and services produced can vary in response to other changes in the economy, including changes in the money supply. We are never very far from

the problem of which change will be dominant, price changes or quantity changes. The different possibilities are connected with variations in the speed at which money circulates. This in turn reflects the desires of the public to hold money balances and their reasons for demanding money.

*If the speed at which money circulates changes, then it is conceivable that neither output nor prices change when the money supply changes. If money continues to circulate at the same rate and output does not change, then prices will rise when more money is available. Any effect that the amount of money in the economy can have on prices must depend on the demand for that money as well as on the supply, since the rate at which money circulates depends on demand relative to supply.*

When we think of the demand for, say, meat, we think of so many pounds per week required for consumption at the going price. This demand is linked directly to 'meat qualities' providing us with satisfaction via meat dinners. The demand for money is rather different. We do not hold so many pounds of meat per week

- to exchange for fish, bus rides and new clothes
- as a means of accumulating a deposit on a new house
- in case of the possible sudden breakdown of our car
- in the expectation that a certain company's shares will fall in price and we can snap them up cheaply.

Yet we may hold money for all these reasons.

Now holding money is not the exclusive means of storing wealth or of meeting the possibility of unforeseen expenditures. We could hold unit trusts or antique furniture for such purposes. But unlike other alternatives, money is the only commodity that performs both these functions *and* serves as a general means of payment – as an immediate claim to goods and services.

It is clearly a matter of choice as to what proportion of our wealth we hold as money, just as it is a matter of choice what proportion we hold as unit trusts or antiques or in any other form. Wealth is accumulated spending power. Money is wealth in its most 'spendable' form. This fact will influence our choice about forms of wealth holding.

*The demand for money is simultaneously a demand for a form of wealth and for a means of immediate payment.*

WHAT DETERMINES THE DEMAND FOR MONEY?

For the most part, income reaches us in the form of money. (People do receive payments in non-money form – as bonus issues of shares, discounts on their firms' goods, etc.). Each of us has spending and saving plans for that money income. To fulfil our spending plans money is *eventually* required as the means of payment. The greater the money value of our spending plans, the larger the volume of money we must hold at one time or another to make eventual payment.

Economists trying to predict the demand for money and reasoning that planned spending depends on income have tried using the behaviour of aggregate income to explain the behaviour of the demand for money. But while there seem to be good grounds for believing that the demand for money increases with planned spending, we would not expect the link between the two to be a rigid one. Allowance must be made for money's other role, as one among many possible forms of wealth.

The alternative to expenditure on current consumption is saving. We receive income as money but may choose to hold part of that income for future consumption expenditure. If we choose not to hold it as money, we make that money available to someone else. For instance, if we use it to buy shares in a newly formed company we are providing that company with immediate purchasing power. If we lend it to the government by purchasing government bonds, we are furnishing the government with the means for some of its expenditures. In each case we are saving it for our own future use.

These choices involve the surrender of money's convenience – its 'spendability' or 'liquidity'. In return for this surrender we expect and receive some form of interest payment. Those wanting money *now* pay interest in one form or another to those who are prepared not to exercise their purchasing power until *later*.

From what we have learned about demand in general, it will not be surprising that relative prices have a part to play in the demand for money. The relative prices here are the rates of interest to be had on alternative assets to money. This interest is sacrificed when money is held instead. The price of monetary convenience is the interest foregone. But if other assets bear a rate of interest and money does not, why bother to hold money at all? Why not simply enjoy the dividends on shares or the interest on a loan to the local authority and cash these assets in as required for spending?

The answer lies in the costs and possible risks attached to converting money into other assets and back again. Stockbrokers have to be paid for buying and selling shares. Perhaps the shares have to be sold below the price at which they were bought to provide instantly needed cash. The same applies to other types of asset – property and the like. We can expect people to weigh the gains from interest payments (and possible appreciation in value) against the costs of not having enough ready cash, when they are deciding what fraction of their wealth to hold in money form. Furthermore, we would expect rising interest rates to have a depressive effect on the demand for money, since money in hand becomes a relatively more expensive form of wealth holding under these conditions.

The behaviour of prices will influence people's attitudes to money holding. As we are all only too well aware, general price rises diminish the real value (purchasing power) of money. People anticipate the rate at which prices are likely to rise and adjust their money-holding behaviour accordingly. For example, if they think the price of houses is going to rise, they will buy houses immediately rather than saving their money in money form. Rapid inflation will produce attempts to economise on cash holding. More of this in a moment.

The larger the money value of transactions we take part in, the larger the amount of money that passes through our hands. We need money at the instant we complete a purchase. But the amount we hold is a matter of choice. Only part of the money we hold this week need be for this week's purchases. Some of it is held as part of overall wealth, the title to future consumption. Even the amount we hold for completing current purchases is not rigidly tied to the value of those transactions. If prices are rising we might reasonably seek to economise on holding large sums of money (which is losing its real value) by making more frequent and smaller shopping expeditions instead of less frequent and larger ones, spending money as it becomes available rather than holding it. Its convenience value is being partly offset by its loss in purchasing power.

Rising prices have conflicting effects on the amount of money we hold. On the one hand, the fact that we have to transact a higher money value of business encourages us to hold larger sums for that very purpose. On the other hand, the fact that money is losing its real value produces attempts to economise on money holding and also encourages conversion from money into alternative assets.

*The demand for money is the product of a quite complex interaction of effects from plans and expectations about spending, interest rates and price behaviour.*

IN WHAT WAY CAN IMBALANCE BETWEEN MONEY SUPPLY AND MONEY DEMAND BE INFLATIONARY?

It seems that the demand for and supply of money can get out of balance just like any other good or service. If the supply of money is being expanded at a different rate to the demand for it, people will find themselves holding different amounts of money from the desired level. If prices change in an unanticipated way this can upset the balance between money supply and demand.

When people have not got what they want they try to change things. So it is with money. If I have the responsibility of running a business and find that too high a proportion of the company's assets is in the form of cash, I try to change the situation. I supply cash in exchange for something else. By doing this I am simultaneously demanding that 'something else' – be it new equipment, shares in another company or whatever.

If this state of affairs is widespread in the economy there will be concerted attempts to unload money for goods or assets. Thus, one theory maintains, if the existing stock of money is different from the desired stock, its rate of circulation will change as people try to adjust the amount they hold to the desired amount. But because these attempts at adjustment inevitably involve transactions in other goods and securities, we can expect their prices to change as the demand for them alters relative to the supply.

*One aspect of inflation is an imbalance between desired and actual money holdings. Such a situation can produce pressure on prices as people alter their spending behaviour in trying to adjust their money balances.*

The fact that *not everyone* can successfully change his money holdings without bringing about additional changes in the economy provides the basis of the change.

We live in a monetary economy. The rising prices that we talk about in discussing inflation are prices in terms of the money unit (£). The spending behaviour of individual members of our economy is ultimately a monetary phenomenon. But supply and demand relationships for money do not tell the whole inflation story. We have witnessed how a discrepancy between *desired* and *actual* money holdings can produce price level changes. This discrepancy can also be a response to price changes. It is time to widen the debate about inflation and to place monetary effects in a broader setting. Money flows are only one view of an exchange mechanism, the other part of which involves flows of goods and services. Monetary changes are themselves partly the *effect* of other disturbances.

# 6

# 'EMPLOYERS' ASSOCIATION DENOUNCES EXCESSIVE WAGE CLAIMS AS INFLATIONARY'

# 'TRADES UNION CONGRESS CALLS FOR PRICE CONTROLS AS FIRST STEP TO HALTING INFLATION'

CAN WE ISOLATE THE BLAME FOR INFLATION AND ATTACH IT TO EITHER UNION OR BUSINESS BEHAVIOUR?

The facts of the inflation of the last twenty years or so are that both prices and money wages have risen. There is no clear evidence that wages have lagged behind prices. Labour's share (in the sense of the value of wages paid out) of the value of aggregate production has, if anything, risen slightly. The amount of money in the economy has continued to increase but not at a constant rate.

A long, confusing and often fruitless debate has accompanied the inflation, encouraged from time to time by the vested interests of labour and business each trying to lodge the 'blame' for inflation squarely in the other's camp. Here is a sample of the opposing arguments put in their crudest terms.

*The employers' view – union aggression*
'The militancy of trade unions has meant that in their efforts to force a redistribution of income away from profits and in favour of wage incomes, they have acted in the sale of labour to somehow force higher wage claims on producers. As producers, impotent to resist and striving to protect profits, experience the increased costs, they reluctantly pass them on to consumers in the form of higher prices.'

*The unions' view – business aggression*
'Because much business is not competitive – it has the ability to *set* prices rather than having to take whatever prices the market decrees for what it produces – it has been using its price-setting power to jack up prices in an effort to obtain a larger share for profit. Price increases are then followed up by understandable union attempts to protect the *real value* of their wages in the face of imposed price increases.'

Variations on these themes have provided the sort of ammunition flung at opposing sides in the efforts of business groups and unions to dissociate themselves from the responsibility for inflation and its consequences. Both groups insist that their part in the inflationary spiral has been a purely defensive one. There are good reasons for rejecting this and for believing that both groups have acted aggressively in the knowledge that their actions would be abetted, if not aided, by the government of the day.

*Neither union nor business aggression can be isolated as the single inflationary cause.*

If business enterprises are indeed trying to maximise profits, indulgence in willy-nilly price increases will not serve this end. In the absence of changes in the economy that bring about increases in the demand for their products at *existing* prices, any attempt to raise prices above this current profit maximising level would simply result in a reduction in sales and a fall in profits.

*Firms will not initiate price increases if these cannot be sustained by shifts in demand for their products.*

IS IT TRUE THAT UNION PRESSURE FOR HIGHER WAGES INEVITABLY LEADS TO INFLATED PRICES?

No-one is likely to contest that when a wage increase is successfully negotiated, and is passed on in the form of price increases then an inflationary event has occurred. *However, it is dangerous to infer that unions have in their grasp the power to force sustained cost increases come what may. They are limited by the countervailing power of firms to resist wage claims. Ultimately the unions are limited by the possibility of increased unemployment among their members, if increased wages bring increased prices and price increases lead to reduced sales.* A shift in demand is needed if this sort of inflation is to be perpetuated, otherwise men are sacked and the union pressure becomes partly self-defeating.

It has probably occurred to the reader that increased money wage claims of the size recently requested in this country – claims for 20 per cent increases and more – even when successful, do not measure the *real* gains to union members because of subsequent inflation. But union leaders are not fools and they are not beguiled into thinking that a 20 per cent wage increase is an improvement in real terms. What they *do* know is that in an economy where *real output* is growing as a result of productivity increases, their members have come to expect a share of this growth. They have no means of ensuring this share through lower prices – *they* don't set the prices. Money wage claims are their means of securing part of the 'spoils of growth'.

This method doesn't work nearly so evenly as price reductions would. Differing union strengths can result in marked inequalities of achievement in the wage bargaining field. There is also a certain amount of *competitive* wage bidding, with unions trying to protect their workers' place on the ladder. It may often be true that union officials don't look so much to their real wage as to their *relative* wage.

Unions would be unlikely to make continual increased money wage claims if substantial unemployment seemed a likely consequence. However, since they cannot count on price *decreases* to confer the benefits of productivity increases on them, they do use money wage claims to try to fulfil their expectations about increasing real incomes.

In answering the last series of questions one common feature has emerged. Whether price increases are *initiated* by firms or whether they are reactions to wage pressure, they have to be *sustained* by shifts in demand. If prices are rising and output and employment are not falling, then aggregate demand or expenditure in money terms is also rising. Inflation has to be financed somehow. Increased spending on higher priced goods is not possible without changes in the means of payment.

But it is one thing to say that *monetary changes* are *necessary* if inflation is to occur and quite another to say that *monetary* expansion *causes* the inflation. It is a different thing again to suggest that rigid control of the money supply is a potential weapon for controlling inflation.

# 'CITY ACCUSES GOVERNMENT OF IRRESPONSIBLE MONETARY POLICY'

EVEN IF INFLATION HAS BEEN 'FACILITATED' BY INCREASES IN THE MONEY SUPPLY, WOULD MONETARY RESTRICTION DEFEAT IT?

This question contains within it two others. Is it possible to effectively control the money supply? If it *is* possible, will this in turn make possible the sort of control of *transactions* in the economy necessary to arrest inflation?

We will concern ourselves with the second point. Even if the government imposes restrictions on the supply of cash and expansion of bank loans, it still has to contend with the ingenuity of the spending public. And it is probably true to say that if there is a high demand for the services of money, people will find ways around the obstacle of a restricted money

70

supply. Although the banking system *appears* to be a financial cornerstone, firms *can* do business on mutually agreed credit terms. This trade credit can expand. Conceivably, credit slips could come to circulate in the economy as a sort of 'parallel money supply'.

Much of the potential to control inflation through controlling the money supply depends on the *confidence* of the spending public in the probable success of such measures. Money really only enjoys its position as the means of payment *par excellence* because of the lesser confidence placed in other forms of payment.

There are some notable instances in history of spectacular failures of confidence in the money of the day. Post First World War Germany saw the virtual failure of currency to finance transactions (barter became common) in a situation of runaway inflation. There have also been marked collapses of confidence in currencies in international exchange.

Some emphasis has been placed on the impact of monetary restrictions on rates of interest. The availability of money for loans relative to the demand for such loans will influence interest rates. Hopefully for monetary policy, measures to raise interest rates would encourage saving out of current income and help to deter investment financed out of borrowed funds, which is made more expensive. Unfortunately, whatever effects there may be seem to take so long to make themselves felt that this kind of manipulation is outdated before it begins to work. Some of the strongest criticisms of using monetary supply changes as a weapon for controlling the economy are based on the long lag in its effectiveness.

*While monetary restriction could conceivably put obstacles in the way of inflation, there is no reason to suppose that it could, on its own, defeat it.*

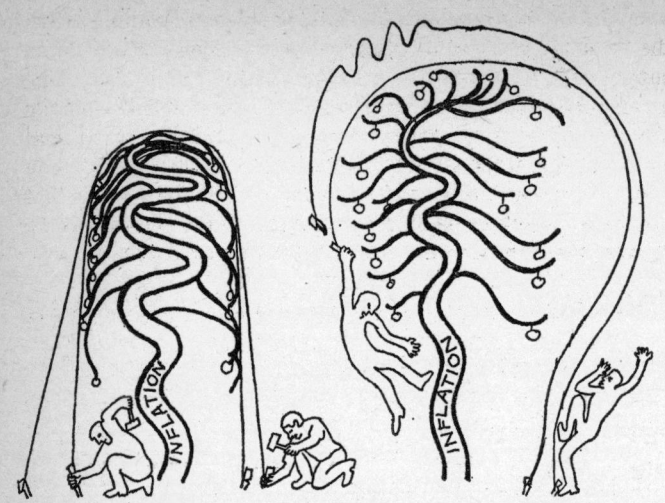

# 'THE DEVIL OF INFLATION OR
# THE DEEP OF UNEMPLOYMENT?'

CAN A LOWER RATE OF INFLATION ONLY BE BOUGHT AT THE
EXPENSE OF HIGHER RATES OF UNEMPLOYMENT?

A considerable weight of historical evidence has been produced pointing to some kind of 'trade-off' between inflation
and unemployment. According to some interpretations of the
evidence, lower and lower unemployment rates are only possible if higher and higher rates of inflation are tolerated. It is
suggested by some that the authorities are political captives to
the idea of full employment, and continual sacrifices have to
be made in the form of price and wage increases. Monetary
authorities will be forced to finance aggregate expenditure
levels that ensure high levels of employment which are incompatible with stable wages and prices.

By what mechanism would such an unfavourable trade-off
develop? In the words of A. W. Phillips, who focused the

attention of the economics profession on the dilemma, 'When the demand for a commodity or service is *high* relative to the supply of it, we expect the price to rise, the rate of rise being greater the greater the *excess demand*'. (Our italics – 'excess demand' means that demand at a given price is higher than supply at that price.) This principle has been applied to rising wage rates and the excess demand for labour. Notice that although the relationship is described in terms of wage rates, price increases have come to be linked with wage rises.

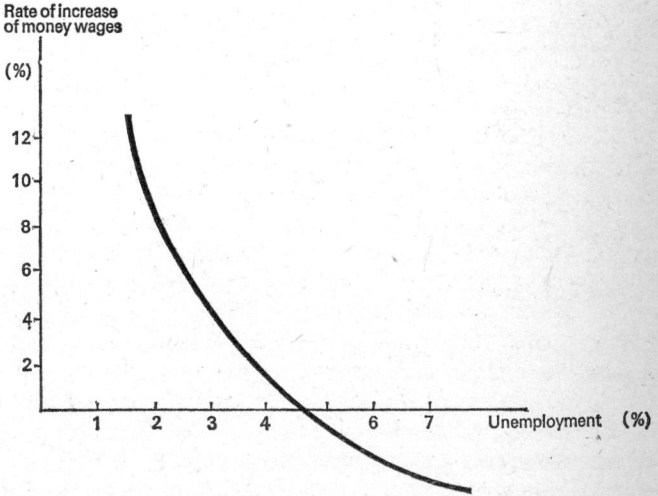

Fig. 4

What are we to make of this term 'excess demand for labour'? The presence of an excess demand for labour supposedly accounts for rises in money wage rates, and the greater the excess demand the more rapid the rise. But Britain has had, in recent years, *positive* levels of unemployment and rapidly rising prices. Does demand really exceed supply if there are dole queues?

Because of imperfect information as to job opportunities, the cost of moving from one occupation to another and the like, some 'frictional' unemployment is inevitable. An excess demand for labour is more accurately reflected in a comparison of positions vacant and the number of people seeking work, making some allowance for the *immobility* of labour in our economy. There will never be completely full employment. We speak of an excess demand when vacancies exceed numbers looking for work. Unemployment will typically be low when excess demand is high. Because unemployment is easier to measure than the more complicated 'excess demand', unemployment has been used in explanations.

*If low levels of unemployment are associated with* HIGH *levels of excess demand for labour, and high excess demand for labour means rapid wage inflation, then low unemployment will be associated with high rates of inflation.*

But we cannot conclude, as many policy-makers have, that simply encouraging unemployment will achieve wage–price stability. As we shall see, the trade-off between inflation and unemployment may be influenced by the rate of inflation which people *expect*. If this expectation is increasing even as more unemployment is being deliberately created, the policy of longer dole queues may not have its desired effect in controlling the growth of prices and wages.

It seems that 'high' employment levels and rapid inflation *do* go together. This does not mean, however, that there are no avenues for altering this relationship.

HOW DO PEOPLE'S EXPECTATIONS ABOUT THE RATE OF INFLATION INFLUENCE THE SITUATION?

Inflation is accompanied by *uncertainty*. It represents people with an additional set of considerations which would not arise in long periods of stable prices. In deciding how to allocate their incomes, both among goods and between present spending and saving, householders may no longer simply consider present prices. Inflation involves a consideration of *future* prices and the rate at which those prices are likely to rise.

If we were all in the happy position of being perfect forecasters, all our spending and saving plans would be fulfilled. In the absence of such perfection, the best we can do is form some *expectation* or *prediction* about future price levels and base our allocation plans on these predictions.

In introducing the role of prices, we examined a simple once-and-for-all rise in prices and glanced at some of its possible effects on householders. There we viewed people as reacting to a change in the price level which had *already* come about. No *further* price changes were envisaged. But in the presence of *persistently* rising prices, people may incorporate predictions about this inflation in their decisions, predictions which may well turn out to be wrong!

*If predictions about inflation prove incorrect, we can expect people, after a time, to revise their expectations and change their allocation decisions.*

If the rate of inflation last year was 8 per cent and people only
expected it to be 5 per cent, painful experience will be likely
to cause them to change their predictions as to this year's rate.

So long as the actual rate of inflation (say 8 per cent) is
*higher* than people expect (say 5 per cent) it will be easier, in
terms of unemployment, to reduce that actual rate than when

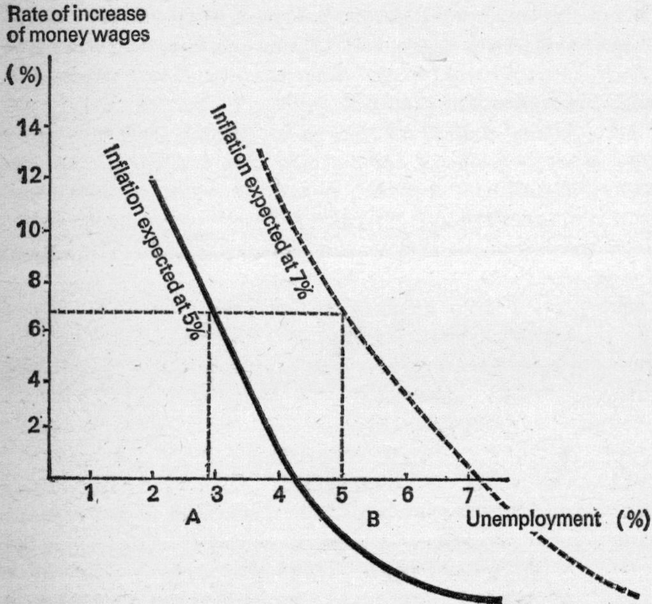

**Rate of increase
of money wages**

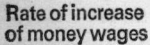

Fig. 5

people have revised their expectations to a higher level (say
7 per cent).

Putting the same point slightly differently, if people *expect*
5 per cent inflation rather than 7 per cent, then inflation can
be contained at 5 per cent with less unemployment than if 7
per cent were expected.

76

The reasoning behind this is as follows. Labour supply and demand are related through the *real wage* (money wages divided by prices). Unemployment is therefore related to the real wage. *Money* wages are negotiated partly on expectations about *future* behaviour of prices. If workers expect a higher level of *price* inflation, *at the current level of unemployment*, this will be reflected in their wage claims. A higher rate of wage inflation will be necessary to keep *real wages* steady and therefore keep unemployment at its *present* level. Referring to Figure 5, the line representing the relationship between the rate of wage increase and unemployment shifts to the right as people come to expect a 7 per cent rate of price inflation. An unemployment rate of B rather than A is then necessary to keep inflation at the 5 per cent level.

*If money wage rates adjust to the expected rate of price inflation, the expectation of faster price rises will bring more rapid wage rises at present levels of unemployment. To reduce actual inflation in these circumstances requires additional unemployment.*

IS IT POSSIBLE TO REDUCE HIGH EXPECTED LEVELS OF INFLATION, SINCE THEY SEEM TO HAVE AN ADVERSE EFFECT ON THE INFLATION–UNEMPLOYMENT TRADE-OFF, WITHOUT RESORTING TO PERIODS OF HIGH UNEMPLOYMENT?

*The advocates of Prices and Incomes Policy claim to be able to answer 'yes' to this question.* They agree that price expectations are largely founded in past and present experience of actual prices. They claim that a favourable history of more stable prices (resulting in lower expectations about the inflation rate) can only be provided by policies that induce higher unemployment, *unless* the price and wage-generating mechanisms are interfered with by legislation or other means. If price and wage inflation is artificially maintained at a low level then people will digest this history of prices and modify their predictions about future price behaviour. This would then allow conventional economic policies such as monetary control, taxation and government spending, to operate, after the removal of the constraints on prices and wages, in an environment where the trade-off between inflation and unemployment is more favourable.

At the time of writing such a policy is in operation and its

effectiveness is too early to assess. Until recently it has been considered an emergency policy to be invoked from time to time, when the uncontrolled system seems to be producing undesirably high inflationary expectations. Assessments of the effectiveness of past attempts of this kind have been ambiguous. At worst it may be that such a policy actually causes people to boost their expectations of inflation through their doubts of its effectiveness and in anticipation of a 'catching-up' process in the economy when the policy is removed.

It now seems likely that a prices and incomes policy, in some form, may become a permanent feature of the British economy.

# 7

# 'STABLE PRICES SEEN AS FIRST AIM OF NEW GOVERNMENT'

SHOULD GOVERNMENTS TRY TO STABILISE PRICES IF THE ALTERNATIVE TO FASTER INFLATION IS HIGHER UNEMPLOYMENT?

It is generally recognised that increasing unemployment carries with it many undesirable 'social costs' of idle human resources. The degradation and misery experienced when it reaches the proportions of the 1930s is well documented and will not be discussed here. On the other hand, the energy devoted to policies for reducing inflation, and indeed the space we have committed to discussing it here, suggests that social costs also attach to inflation. The efficiency of the whole exchange mechanism can be impaired with money losing its purchasing power at an increasing rate. Now it is quite conceivable an economist might find that, on efficiency grounds alone, a reduction in the rate of inflation of 4 per cent at the expense of, say, 1 per cent more unemployment, is 'advisable'. (He may refrain from advocating policies to effect this, of course, through moral or other objections to unemployment.)

*It is* conceivable *that inflation, if sufficiently rapid, can cause such distortions that, in terms of economic efficiency, a point is reached where additional inflation adds more to social costs than does the alternative sacrifice in employment.* (Try measuring it!)

HOW ARE THE BENEFITS OF INFLATION DISTRIBUTED?

A large proportion of the unemployed in the economy also belong to the poorest section of the community. Now to the extent that extra inflation is matched by unemployment reduction, there are likely to be effects on the amount of output produced *and* on the distribution of that output among the members of the economy. Any increased earning opportunities among the poorer sections of the community which are not matched elsewhere will change the distribution of income in favour of the poor.

Furthermore, if more rapid inflation is accompanied by lower unemployment, it may reduce the need for some taxes, as fewer people need to be State-supported. So to this extent, the size of the output 'pie' to be distributed will increase. There may also be a reduction in the inefficiency supposedly caused by the disincentive effects of taxes on the taxpayer.

If the unemployed are potential gainers from inflation, there are also losers. Among them are all those for whom some part of the inflation is unexpected. They may lose part of the real value of their wealth as a result of being caught out with more of their wealth in money balances than they would have had, had they been able to accurately predict the inflation.

Another way of incidentally forcing people to have less income to spend is known as 'fiscal drag'. Our income tax system includes higher tax rates at higher *money* income levels. As people move into higher income brackets as part of the inflationary mechanism, they find themselves paying a higher *proportion* of that money income in tax. Inflation therefore produces additional transfers of spending power from individuals to the State.

Those with a disproportionately large amount of their wealth concentrated in the form of loans will suffer accordingly if the interest payments they are to receive do not fully embody 'cover' for the inflation that actually takes place – unless the annual rate of interest is higher than the annual rate of inflation, the lender will lose. A transfer takes place from creditors to debtors, who gain accordingly.

*Inflation brings about distribution effects, some of which are transfers between creditors and debtors, some between the individual and the State, some between the recipients of fixed incomes such as pensioners, and those on unfixed incomes. As an* alternative to unemployment, increased inflation may also bring social benefits by increasing overall output and reducing the weight of inefficiency-inducing taxes.

The 'benefits' of inflation are nearly always indirectly spelled out in terms of the benefits of reduced unemployment. The

'costs' of inflation are more direct. Our attention is continually drawn to the impact of inflation on pensioners. This group is singled out by press and politicians as members of the class drawing incomes fixed in money terms. We have already mentioned other such groups, among them those whose incomes are in the form of interest payments. Pensioners, however, tend to draw attention because, perhaps, of widespread feelings that the present income distribution is undesirable but is being made even worse through inflationary effects.

WHAT ARE THE COSTS OF INFLATION?

*Inefficiency.* Because some part of the current inflation is un-expected there are all sorts of 'costs and adjustments' that ac-company an inflationary situation. When people cannot fully anticipate change, they make mistakes. This uncertainty ac-companying inflation reduces efficiency simply because some of the real resources of the economy are tied up in dealing with it. Policy reviews may be needed more frequently by firms, price lists have to be more frequently revised, and so on. All these are real effects which absorb some of the scarce resources of the economy.

*The rate of inflation relative to that in countries with whom we trade can influence both exports and imports.* If we experience more rapid inflation than our major trading partners this will make our exports *relatively* more expensive and imported goods more attractive to us as they seem relatively cheap. If these effects were allowed to transmit themselves unhindered through the economy they could have *correction* effects on inflation. Unattractively high export prices could reduce export sales and employment in that section of industry with further depressive effects on the domestic economy. Increased spending on imports diverts demand for goods from the domestic economy to foreign ones where those goods are produced, thus lowering the level of aggregate demand in the home economy.

But of course these effects are *not* allowed to work themselves out. These problems lead us naturally into a fuller discussion of the international aspects of our economy.

# 8

# 'TRADE FIGURES REVEAL BRITISH FAILURE IN WORLD MARKETS'

WHY ARE GOODS EXCHANGED BETWEEN COUNTRIES AT ALL? WOULDN'T IT BE BETTER TO BE AS SELF-SUFFICIENT AS POSSIBLE?

Neither you nor I would normally attempt to be self-sufficient. We have different abilities, different tastes in what we want to do, and there are one or two things that we can do much better than anything else. We take advantage of our different endowments of skill to specialise in occupations and use our earnings to buy the goods and services of others who are doing likewise. An organised market structure enables us to pool our resources. In this way, *specialisation increases the overall level of goods available.*

HOW DOES THIS MECHANISM WORK INTERNATIONALLY?

If you were to look at two tables showing the composition of production in Britain and India, you would notice striking differences in the relative importance of many goods in the make-up of the output of each. While it is impractical for countries to specialise completely in the production of one good, it is nevertheless in their interest to practise a degree of specialisation and then trade. This is because countries differ in the relative efficiency with which they can produce different goods.

It would, for example, be foolish for England to try and grow cotton, which requires cheap labour and a hot climate. It would be equally foolish for India to try and grow soft temperate fruits in a tropical climate. The diversion of resources from other uses, necessary to accomplish such a change in production, would be wasteful.

Although most countries could, if necessary, produce most goods, the above example points to the fact that a country will

have a *comparative advantage* over other countries in the production of one or several commodities. What are the consequences of this?

Japan might be able, for example, to produce *all* goods at a lower cost in resources than Thailand. Nevertheless if Thailand is *least inefficient* in its production of rice, then it may benefit both countries for Thailand to concentrate on rice production for export to Japan while Japan specialises in the output of manufactures, some of which can be purchased by Thailand.

If, for instance, in Japan 1 'unit' of that country's resources could produce either 10 'units' of rice or 5 'units' of manufactures while in Thailand only 4 units of rice or 1 unit of manufactures arise from the same resource outlay, we have a case where Japan is absolutely more efficient in both agriculture and manufacturing, but Thailand has a *comparative* advantage in agriculture.

The 'most efficient' use of resources would suggest that Japan transfer out of rice manufacture (it only has to give up 2 units of rice to achieve 1 extra manufacture). Meanwhile Thailand's specialisation in rice would mean a gain of 4 rice units for every manufacture sacrificed.

In the absence of trade the relative price of manufactures in Japan can be measured in terms of the rice foregone and thus the relative price of manufactures in terms of rice is 10 : 5 (or 2 : 1). In Thailand it is 4 : 1. If an international relative price of, say, 3 : 1 was established through trade, both Thailand and Japan would gain as a result. Domestically Japan would have to sacrifice 1 manufacture for only 2 units of rice. Internationally, it can obtain 3. Thailand, in order to produce manufactures at all, has to give up 4 possible units of rice. By trading, it only has to offer 3.

Comparative advantage may not necessarily be permanent. An example of a change can be seen by looking at British history. While Britain could produce cotton goods and ships relatively more cheaply than other countries in the nineteenth century, because of more advanced techniques and knowledge, she could export these easily. However, now that other countries, notably the U.S. and Japan, can produce these more cheaply, it is in the interest of Britain to import these goods and specialise in some other goods in which she has a comparative advantage.

*Fundamentally the international trading mechanism is a large-scale version of the interpersonal trading mechanism.*

# 'WORLD DOLLAR SHORTAGE IN THE FIFTIES: GLUT IN THE SEVENTIES'

WHY IS 'FOREIGN EXCHANGE' IMPORTANT?

If you are, for example, an English textile manufacturer, you will want to be paid for any goods you sell in pounds sterling. French francs would be of little use when it comes to paying wage bills for local workers, interest commitments to local banks, and so on, unless the French franc were acceptable as a medium of exchange in Britain.

A Frenchman wanting to import English textiles would therefore have to acquire pounds sterling in order to pay for his purchases.

Similarly English importers wanting to buy French wine will have to acquire French francs to pay the wine manufacturer.

*In the absence of any desire to trade goods or services internationally, there would be no international currency transactions.*

WHO PROVIDES FOREIGN CURRENCY FOR THOSE WHO WANT TO BUY FOREIGN GOODS?

While an Englishman is buying francs from France, which he must do if he wants to buy French goods, he is simultaneously supplying France with pounds sterling.

While a Frenchman is buying pounds from England, he is simultaneously supplying England with French francs.

*The supply of one currency is therefore incidentally included in the demand for another currency. The actual cash is acquired through the international banking system.*

## WHAT HAPPENS TO A COUNTRY'S FOREIGN CURRENCY SUPPLIES IF OTHER COUNTRIES WANT TO BUY LESS OF ITS GOODS?

The supply of and demand for the currencies of various nations are reflections of the underlying supply and demand relationships for goods and services being traded among those nations.

*If there is a fall in the demand for a country's goods, there will be a fall in the demand for its currency and therefore a reduced supply of foreign currencies flowing into that country.*

## WHAT ARE EXCHANGE RATES?

*Exchange rates are prices of currencies in terms of other currencies.*

The price of one currency in terms of another means the number of dollars which can be bought with £1, the number of francs which can be bought with one dollar, and so on. These prices were, for a long time, 'fixed' internationally. At present some are 'floating' but may return to being fixed.

These exchange rates, if they were not in fact 'fixed' by international monetary authorities, would be derived from the demand and supply for trading countries' exports and imports. Changes in export–import patterns, resulting from changes in relative costs in different countries, mean that there would be tendencies for the relative prices of the traded currencies to change. If English knitwear gained in international popularity, there would be an increase in the demand for pounds to enable foreigners to buy the knitwear.

If the Japanese started to produce violins which were comparable in quality with, and cheaper than Italian violins, the demand for yen would rise and the demand for lire would fall, so long as other trade remained undisturbed.

*If exchange rates are allowed to vary without help or hindrance from governments, we have what is known as a flexible or 'floating' exchange rate system. Relative prices of different currencies depend on import–export patterns and change accordingly.*

Before 1972, with few exceptions, it had been the practice of most countries to try to keep the prices of their currencies fixed in terms of others, or to vary them within narrow limits, for fairly long periods.

*Trade takes place for the most part, not between governments, but between individual importers and exporters who use commercial banks as the intermediaries through whom they make and receive payments. The exchange rates would, if flexible, reflect these transactions.*

But governments can act by mutual agreement to limit the fluctuations of these exchange rates through their Central Banks, which are government-controlled institutions. The Bank of England and the Federal Reserve Bank of the United States are examples of such central banks.

*Most exchange rates, until recently, were fixed in this way.*

## HOW CAN GOVERNMENTS, THROUGH THEIR CENTRAL BANKS, STABILISE EXCHANGE RATES?

Let us imagine that the British exchange rates are fixed, i.e. that there is a fixed price for pounds vis-à-vis other curencies, and vice versa. Then let us imagine that there is a change in trading patterns so that the British wish to import an increased number of American goods, but there is no corresponding increase in American imports from Britain.

As a result of the British desire to import more American goods, their demand for dollars rises. Simultaneously the supply of pounds available increases on the foreign exchange markets. If exchange rates were flexible, the price of pounds would fall in terms of dollars, i.e. we could get fewer dollars for each pound.

However, by the agreements which characterise a fixed exchange rate system, exchange rates cannot suddenly change. To maintain the price of the pound and of the dollar, the Central

Banks will intervene. The Bank of England, which keeps some dollars in reserve, uses dollars to buy back sterling.

*This compensating increase in the demand for sterling and increase in the supply of dollars (used to buy sterling) should restore the relative prices of the two currencies to their previously agreed levels.*

# 'GOVERNMENT STEPS IN TO SAVE THE POUND: RESERVES FALL TO A CRITICAL LEVEL'

WHAT ARE THESE RESERVES, AND WHY ARE THEY SO IMPORTANT?

In order for buying and selling of currencies to be possible, the Central Banks must have access to *stocks of foreign currency*. *These stocks are the Foreign Reserves* which receive so much attention in reports on the state of the economy.

When a country's currency is 'strong', i.e. the demand for it is high relative to the supply, the Central Bank can build up its stocks of foreign reserves. When a currency is 'weak', its reserves tend to be depleted.

Under fixed exchange rates, governments use foreign reserves to maintain the agreed exchange rates by altering the demand for, and supply of, their currency. They sell reserves to 'strengthen' their currency, and buy them when demand for their currency is high. Thus these reserves necesarily fluctuate as they are drawn upon or built up.

Foreign reserves play a similar role internationally as a private individual's savings might to him. While the stock of savings is building up, the individual is better equipped both for future consumption and to cope with emergencies. If, however, his stock is running down, he is spending more than his current income, and cannot do so indefinitely. When a country's goods (and currency) are in demand, therefore, the stock is being replenished. Once a country's stock of reserves has run out, that country no longer has the power to maintain demand for its currency to keep it at the agreed level.

*Under a fixed exchange rate system, reserves are needed to maintain exchange prices of currencies. But the existence of a stock of foreign reserves loses much of its importance under a flexible exchange rate system, because there is no longer any need to maintain particular exchange rates.*

One of the reasons why the fixed exchange rate system more or less collapsed in 1973 was that countries were, partly through a shortage of reserves, no longer able to support their currencies.

HOW DO FLEXIBLE EXCHANGE RATES WORK?

When the demand for a country's goods falls, the demand for its currency will fall. So the price of its currency will fall in terms of that of other currencies. The country whose currency has experienced a fall in demand will therefore find imports relatively more expensive, and its residents will try to substitute home produced goods for some imports.

This will result in a fall in the supply of its currency on world markets, which will help prevent a further fall in its price.

*Flexible exchange rates adjust automatically to changes in the pattern of imports and exports.*

In June 1972, the British Government was under strong foreign
pressure to try and find an exchange rate for the pound at a
level which was a closer reflection of the underlying demand
and supply relationships than it had been up to that date.

The Government therefore decided to temporarily suspend
the rule that the rate of exchange could only fluctuate within
limits of 2 per cent around the agreed rate. It was to be allowed
to fluctuate within very much broader limits (which were not
publicly stated), until it 'settled down'. It was intended to be
only temporary; six months was considered long enough.

The limits, even if not publicly stated, become clear when
the Bank of England intervenes. The pound exchanged at a
price of about 2.50 dollars in June, but by October, when it
looked as if it might drop below 2.35, the Bank of England
stepped in to support it. The support was, however, not consistent, but was given at times when panic selling of the pound
seemed a possibility.

*The exchange rate in Britain in 1972, while allowed to fluctu-
ate, was therefore not completely flexible; this was shown by
the Bank of England's intervention.*

(We should note that at the time of writing (1973), the pound
has been 'floating' for a year, together with several other currencies. The present government does not appear to be treating
refixing it as an urgent priority.)

International trading of goods and services is not the only form
of international exchange. There are also transactions of a
different kind known as 'capital movements'.

If a British businessman decides to invest in an Australian

91

mining company he is, incidentally, providing Australia with additional sterling.

*This is a capital movement, and also affects the demand for and supply of currencies.*

WHAT EFFECT DO CAPITAL MOVEMENTS HAVE ON CURRENCY PRICES?

If Australia imports goods and services to a value greater than the value of its exports, it is increasing the demand for other currencies and increasing the supply of Australian dollars. This would tend to lead to a fall in the exchange price of the Australian dollar, or under a fixed exchange rate system, a fall in foreign reserves.

However, if Britain, America or other countries invest in Australia, this will increase the supply of foreign currencies to Australia and tend to offset the effect of the increased supply of Australian dollars.

It could also be the case that Australians invested their capital abroad. This would result in an increase in the supply of Australian dollars to those countries in which they invested.

*Capital movements can therefore either compensate for currency movements and strengthen currency prices, or they can reinforce currency movements and weaken currency prices.*

# 9

# 'BRITAIN MAY BE FORCED TO DEVALUE TO SOLVE BALANCE OF PAYMENTS PROBLEM'

WHAT IS THE BALANCE OF PAYMENTS?

The term 'balance of payments' tends to be used loosely in reports on the economy. We shall look at various definitions.

The country has two accounts, labelled 'current' and 'capital'. The *current* account records current payments for exports and imports of goods and services. These exports and imports are further divided into two categories, 'visible' and 'invisible' goods and services. In the 'visible' category come goods which, basically, have to be physically exported and imported. (Technically, it includes all those goods which have to be cleared through Customs.) It includes food, clothing, machinery, etc. Into the invisible category come services such as shipping, insurance, international banking facilities, brokerage fees in foreign stock transactions and anything else which does not have to be cleared through Customs.

The *capital* account records movements of capital (in the financial sense), both long and short term. For example, when a British insurance company makes a loan to an Australian company, this transaction is recorded as an outflow on the British capital account. When an Australian buys pounds to invest in a British Unit Trust, the transaction is recorded as an inflow on the British capital account.

The *balance* of the account means the difference between incoming and outgoing payments. When more is coming in than going out, the account is said to be in surplus. When more is being paid out than received, the account is said to be in deficit.

When incoming payments equal outgoing revenue, the account is in balance.

By definition, payments must always balance, although each separate account may show a deficit or surplus. Any imbalance is made good through alterations in the level of reserves. In the case of a deficit, balance is achieved by using the country's foreign reserves or by borrowing the money from private individuals, countries or the International Monetary Fund.

We frequently hear about the Balance of Trade. This is normally a reference to the account for visible trade. *The term 'balance of payments', correctly used, means the difference between imports and exports on both the capital and current accounts.*

WHY SHOULD A BALANCE OF PAYMENTS DEFICIT BE A PROBLEM?

A balance of payments deficit problem can be characterised as a persistent tendency for the imports of a country to exceed its exports. This means that there will be excess supply of the deficit country's currency. Under a fixed exchange rate system, that country will continually be depleting its reserves.

Under a flexible exchange rate system, the problem does not arise because the price of a country's currency will automatically adjust to reflect demand and supply conditions and ensure an automatic balance. But the effects of such an automatic balancing procedure are felt *elsewhere* in the economy.

Under a fixed exchange rate system this automatic adjustment does not take place and, should a balance of payments deficit problem arise, the deficit country normally finds it necessary to take measures to cut back the total level of expenditure, thus incidentally lowering its expenditure on imports.

*Balance of payments deficits, if persistent, imply that the deficit country is not 'paying its way' in world markets, and is living 'above its income'.*

If, as a result of trading activities, a country is persistently exporting a greater value of goods than it is importing and is acquiring an increasing store of foreign exchange as a result, this foreign currency is being *held* and not *spent*. This means that the surplus country is postponing the use of its claims to

foreigners' goods and services (this is what a stock of foreign currency represents).

Since in economics we often equate increased consumption with increased welfare, the accumulation of *claims* on foreign resources does not benefit the surplus country's inhabitants until these claims are spent.

A surplus country is in fact giving other countries the right to postpone payments for their own imports. Eventually these countries may have to reduce their level of imports, which may include the surplus country's exports, in an attempt to balance their accounts and avoid international bankruptcy.

*A surplus, if continued, lowers the possible standard of living of the surplus country's inhabitants. It is unlikely that other countries will allow it to continue indefinitely.*

Since the war Britain has used devaluation twice (in 1949 and 1967) to try to correct a balance of payments deficit which arose in the context of the fixed exchange rate system operating at those times.

*A currency devaluation amounts to the declaration of a new, lower rate of exchange at which the country's currency will exchange for that of foreigners.*

Britain devalued the pound sterling in 1967 when it declared that the Bank of England would no longer support the price of sterling at £1 exchanging for $2.80, but would in future 'support' it at $2.40. Fewer dollars were required to purchase a British pound and the British pound would exchange for fewer dollars.

## HOW COULD THIS DEVALUATION HELP THE BALANCE OF PAYMENTS PROBLEM?

If, after a devaluation, British manufacturers still offer their goods at pre-devaluation sterling prices to American importers, those importers will be able to purchase them for a smaller number of dollars than before.

If there are alternative supplies of similar goods available in America, the British versions are now relatively cheaper. We might expect the American public to buy more of them. Exactly how much more they buy will depend on the extent of the devaluation, and on how sensitive American consumers are to the change in relative prices.

*As long as the Americans increase the value of their purchases, the demand for pounds and supply of dollars will rise, thus benefiting British foreign reserves.*

But even though Americans buy more goods, the total value (price of goods multiplied by quantity sold) of their expenditure on British goods could fall.

If, as in 1966, the £ were worth $2.80 and an American firm was importing 500 Shetland sweaters at £2 each, then the *dollar* value of those British exports was $2,800. Now, if as in 1967, the pound was devalued so that £1 = $2.40, the dollar price of a sweater has fallen from $5.60 to $4.80. But if the Americans still want only 500 sweaters, the dollar value of those exports will fall to $2,400. Even if, because of the reduced

dollar price, the Americans purchase 550 sweaters, dollar earning for Britain on account of the sweaters will still be only $2,640, which is $160 *less* than before devaluation.

*If the value of exports from Britain is not increased, the total demand for pounds will not increase and devaluation will have been ineffective in this respect.*

This analysis is based on the assumption that, as demand for British goods rises, production can increase to meet this demand without the price of the products having to increase significantly. Devaluation has had an effect on imports into Britain in that American products have become relatively more expensive for English consumers, who may therefore buy fewer American goods.

*Provided the* TOTAL VALUE *of imports falls (which is not necessarily the case even if the volume falls), the demand for dollars and supply of pounds will fall.*

(I) We have assumed that, after a devaluation, British exporters would not change the price of their goods. However, many exports require imported products for use in the process of their manufacture, for example cotton textiles. If these imported products come from countries whose currencies have become dearer in pounds as a result of a devaluation of the pound, the costs of the British exporters may have increased, which could lead them to increase their prices.

(II) Unless the devaluation is internationally agreed, which it usually is, *other countries may retaliate by also devaluing*, to restore their competitive advantage.

This retaliation may nullify the effect of one country's devaluation.

(III) *The ultimate effects of the devaluation take some time to work through international markets. There may be many reactions to the changes in relative prices, caused by devaluation, which cannot be predicted.*

## HOW CAN SURPLUS COUNTRIES REMEDY THEIR DIFFICULTIES?

If a country is in surplus it can revalue its currency. The effect is precisely the opposite of devaluation: *instead of lowering the price of its currency, the revaluing country raises the price of its currency.*

If the measure is successful, there will be a fall in demand for the revalued currency. There should also be a fall in demand for the revaluing country's exports, and a rise in its imports, as foreign goods become relatively cheaper.

# 'STOP–GO POLICIES ARE BACK: SQUEEZE EXPECTED SOON'

## IS DEVALUATION THE ONLY SOLUTION TO A BALANCE OF PAYMENTS DEFICIT PROBLEM?

There are various domestic policies that a government may undertake. Rather than changing the relative prices of internationally traded goods by devaluation, a government may act to reduce the volume of imports indirectly by exerting pressure on the level of domestic spending, by, for example, restricting credit to reduce demand.

The change in international relative prices may be due to inflation. If Britain is inflating faster than its major trading partners, the relative increase in the prices of its goods may be at the root of a persistent balance of payments deficit.

*In this case, anti-inflation measures such as taxation meas-*

*ures, credit curbs, and restrictions on government expenditure may be used.*

If such measures were successful they would reduce the level of aggregate demands and aggregate incomes. Since imports depend on aggregate income, they too would be reduced.

At the same time, the level of British prices would be stabilised. This might help to stop any further reduction in exports. There would also be an increase in demand for home produced goods, since the stabilisation of home prices will encourage people to buy home produced instead of foreign goods.

Deflationary policies may include measures to limit credit. This also causes a reduction in aggregate demand. It may incidentally have adverse effects in the long run due to the fall in investment.

*As a last resort the government can impose tariffs on foreign goods entering the country.* Since such tariffs raise the prices of these goods in the shops, they are likely to divert consumption away from foreign goods and towards relatively cheaper, home produced goods. The extent to which a country can put tariffs on imports is limited by what foreign reaction is likely to be. On the whole, tariffs are unpopular because they tend to damp down the flow of trade.

Further, most non-communist countries belong to the General Agreement on Tariffs and Trade (GATT). This organisation is attempting to reduce barriers to international trade. In general, a country will not impose tariffs unless, as required by GATT, all other parties to the agreement are consulted. Thus, countries are encouraged to pursue mutually beneficial tariff policies.

*The most effective way of dealing with a balance of payments deficit is unlikely to be through either devaluation or domestic policies alone.* Devaluation is unlikely to have the desired effects unless supported by the domestic policies mentioned. The degree of deflation necessary to cure a deficit problem, without devaluing, could lead to drastic unemployment which is considered socially and politically undesirable.

# 'REPORT RECOMMENDS THE ADOPTION OF FLEXIBLE EXCHANGE RATES'

WHY ARE FLEXIBLE EXCHANGE RATES GAINING FAVOUR?

A flexible exchange rate system is one in which exchange rates are not fixed but may fluctuate with changes in the demand and supply for the various currencies. The demands for, and supplies of, these currencies will reflect the underlying demand and supply relationships for goods and services in different countries. If, for example, the demand for British goods falls, the price of the pound would fall, provided of course there are no other changes at the time which might affect the price of the pound.

Britain would be able to import less goods and might export more, if the fall in the price of the pound made her goods sufficiently competitive. They would be 'sufficiently competitive' if demand for the goods rose to make the value of exports (price × quantity sold) equal to the value of imports. However, imports would at the same time be reduced as they would be relatively more expensive than before.

The price of the pound would continue to fall until the

value of exports was equal to the value of imports. This adjustment of exports and imports would involve changes in the demand and supply patterns for goods and services in Britain.

*Flexible exchange rates could thus automatically eliminate balance of payments deficits or surpluses.*

IF THERE IS SUCH AN EASY SOLUTION TO BALANCE OF PAYMENTS PROBLEMS, WHY HAS IT NOT YET BEEN PERMANENTLY ADOPTED?

Problems would arise for some international deals as a result of fluctuating exchange rates. When a buyer from America, for example, does not know what the pound and dollar prices

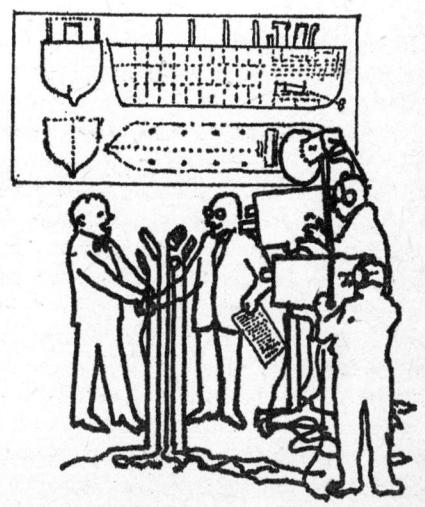

of a good will be a year hence when he requires the goods, his purchasing decision will be complicated. However, an American oil company wishing to take delivery of a British-built tanker, costing £1m. a year hence, could deal with the problem of a fluctuating exchange rate between pound and dollar in the following way: It could arrange for its bankers to '*buy forward*', paying dollars for £1m. which will be made available in a year's time. The point is that the risk of pounds becoming more expensive in the meantime is avoided by paying over dollars at an exchange rate agreed *now*. Of course if pounds should become cheaper in the meantime, that is bad luck for the oil company. That would favour the people who are *selling pounds forward*, who are gambling on just this eventuality, and who will then buy them cheaply to honour obligations to provide pounds just as they become due. Nevertheless, it *is* possible to guard against required foreign currencies becoming unduly dear by 'buying forward'.

Another problem is that flexible exchange rates could aggravate domestic inflation or deflation. Consider a country which relies to a great extent on imported raw materials and foodstuffs. The demand for these commodities is not much influenced by their price, since alternative sources of supply of these necessities don't exist.

If this country's exchange rate falls, it will continue to buy the foodstuffs and raw materials at the new, relatively higher price. The resulting increase in raw material costs will drive up the price of finished goods. This could lead to 'compensating' wage claims. If an inflationary situation now sets in, prices will continue to rise, exports will continue to fall, and the exchange rate will fall again; the whole process could then be repeated.

There would, therefore, for a country such as Britain, be as great a need as there is at present for effective control of prices and wages.

*It is not yet clear precisely what the effects of a flexible exchange rate system would be, and how it would affect trade, inflation and employment. There remains considerable doubt as to its efficacy. This doubt has discouraged its adoption.*

# 'CAN WORLD CURRENCY CRISIS BE AVERTED?'

IT SEEMS THAT MANY COUNTRIES HAVE CURRENCY AND BALANCE OF PAYMENTS PROBLEMS AT THE MOMENT. CAN WE REALLY REGARD EACH COUNTRY'S PROBLEMS AS PARTICULAR TO ITSELF?

It has been suggested that rather than treating each country independently, we should examine the total world situation. We can draw a parallel with our previous discussion of inflation, in which we saw that if the supply of money in a country expanded faster than productivity, prices would tend to rise. If we simply apply this to the whole Western world, we can see that since the Second World War, the world supply of money has risen relative to the growth of world productivity. So we might conclude that here could be a possible source of the problem.

Furthermore, if one country is suffering from inflation, and exchange rates are fixed, trade between countries may tend to spread the inflation as the price of goods to importing countries rises, raising their general levels of prices.

On the other hand, deflationary policies by one country which lower the level of money demand in that country, and may effectively put money in the hands of other countries (perhaps by slowing down investment at home and thus encouraging people to invest abroad), may not only increase their own unemployment, but could well aggravate the problems of inflation elsewhere.

Each country's place in the world economy gives it some influence on every other country's monetary system, and thereby its whole economy. So any analysis which treats each country's economy's problems as specific only to that country, and determined within that country, is likely to be incomplete.

To date, 'world-wide' analysis has not been the normal way

of looking at this problem. *However, since both balance of payments and their associated inflationary problems are now common to most countries of the Western capitalist world, an international approach seems to merit consideration.*

# 10

# 'BRITISH GROWTH RATE ONLY 2% IN 1970. IS 5% FEASIBLE IN 1974?'

The term 'growth rate' can be, and has been used to mean several different things.

(I) It can refer to the amount, in percentage terms, by which aggregate output (i.e. the total amount of goods and services produced) has increased during a given period, usually a year.

(II) It can refer to the percentage increase in the amount that has been produced per head of population in that period.

(III) It can mean the percentage increase in output per employed worker and, as such, would be equivalent to the growth in *labour productivity*. (Similarly, we could attempt to measure percentage increases in output per unit of capital to obtain a measure of growth in capital productivity. This is less common because of serious difficulties in satisfactorily measuring capital.)

*The 'relevant' growth concept will depend on the economic problem being considered.*

From the point of view of the welfare of the community, growth in terms of aggregate output per head would seem to be more relevant than simply growth of output as such. Increases in production which are more than offset by population increases would not raise the living standards of all members of the economy. We shall see later that even when output per head is increasing, each person's standard of living may not be rising.

We have already mentioned one aspect of growth, in terms of labour productivity, in the question of inflationary wage

claims. This measure of growth also has an important place in the wider debate about labour's share of output in an expanding economy. We cannot pursue those issues here. We can, however, point to some of the sources of growth in labour productivity.

(I) Perhaps the first and most obvious of these is an *improvement in the quality of labour itself*.

(*a*) In some instances this may result simply from labour being healthier. This problem has an element of circularity about it. Growth in output (including food production, health services, etc.) may be itself a pre-condition for improvements in labour productivity.

(*b*) Improvements in the quality of labour also stem from the acquisition of superior skills. The education process is of fundamental importance here.

(II) *The provision of more capital equipment with which to work can also increase output per worker*. This is simply an aspect of the diminishing returns we saw at work in the discussion of labour productivity. If it is true that more labour applied to a fixed amount of capital equipment will eventually lead to diminishing increments in labour's output, then surely *more* capital equipment, or more productive capital equipment, given to a *fixed* amount of labour can help to offset this process.

(III) *The organisation of the work force* can be changed in ways that make it more efficient and more productive, i.e. superior management can help to increase per capita output.

Sources I(*b*), (II) and (III) all involve *investment* of some description, either directly in labour itself as in the case of I(*b*), or through the accumulation of more and better capital equipment as in (II) and (III).

IS INVESTMENT ALONE A SUFFICIENT CONDITION FOR ECONOMIC GROWTH?

While we shall be much concerned with the implications of investment for economic growth, it is important not to lose sight of some of the other major features of a growing economy, and the changes that have accompanied the transformation of less sophisticated communities into modern industrial economies. A brief excursion into British history will serve this second purpose.

The phenomenon of the Industrial Revolution in Britain saw a growth in aggregate output, output per head and output per worker. This growth was at a higher rate, and lasted for a longer period than at any previous time in British history. From about the mid eighteenth century, a rise in the population growth rate was supported by improvements in domestic agricultural and industrial technology and by a dramatic increase in imports. These changes were accompanied by a significant reorganisation of the economic system.

The emergence of a factory system of industrial production to replace the former small-scale cottage industry was accompanied by the *specialisation of labour* not so much along the traditional craft lines but in processes of production. Specialised plant and equipment was also devised on a scale unparalleled in the past.

This specialisation led to increasing sophistication of the

*mechanism of exchange* in the economy. Factory production meant *urbanisation* and urbanisation required improved exchange facilities, so that industrial labour in the towns could be fed and so that industrial products could be distributed to rural consumers.

At the same time, the installation of more and better capital equipment did not take place in an institutional vacuum. Not all the funds required by investors came from their own savings and improvements in *the arrangements co-ordinating borrowers and lenders* of money (e.g. banks) were an integral part of the process of growth.

Reference to the history of our own economy reveals all the important institutional and organisational changes that were required to facilitate growth. The amassing of more and better capital equipment could not have been sustained without those changes. *But while investment activity does not ensure* GROWTH, *it is* NECESSARY *in one form or another, if growth is to occur.*

IF THERE WERE GREAT TECHNOLOGICAL IMPROVEMENTS, WHY WOULD NET INVESTMENT BE NECESSARY TO ACHIEVE ECONOMIC GROWTH?

Technical progress is a source of economic growth. It may allow us to make the same number of goods as before, using fewer resources. It also provides us with new goods, increasing our range of choice. Advocates of a stationary population for Britain might claim that zero population growth would enable the economy to consume all it produces except for 'replacement investment'. The economy could thus grow by simply replacing existing machinery by superior types as the old stock wears out.

The snag is that investment, in the form of research, is necessary to achieve technical progress in the first place. Very few new industrial techniques emerge as the result of 'brainwaves'. Furthermore, new techniques may require an increase of scale of operations for their use. This increase in scale neces-

110

sitates what we have called *net* investment, which means *net additions* to the existing capital stock.

In other words, 'better capital' may often mean more capital. *It follows that the replacement of worn-out capital with new capital does not guarantee growth in output per head even if there is zero population growth.*

IS THERE ANY CONFLICT BETWEEN ACHIEVING A PARTICULAR RATE OF GROWTH AND MAINTAINING FULL EMPLOYMENT?

When the Prime Minister announces that the government is undertaking to achieve a 5 per cent growth rate in the economy, is he secretly acknowledging that this might not be compatible with full employment? He knows that labour already employed in declining industries will be unlikely to be able to move into the new industries, either through lack of the required skills or because of the difficulty of moving geographically. Furthermore, the 'growth' industries may well be capital-intensive and therefore need a proportionately smaller labour input than the old industries.

From what we have seen so far, growth seems intimately connected with the rate of investment. But recall that the level of employment is likewise dependent on investment, since investment plays a part in creating jobs as part of aggregate demand.

Now investment is first and foremost a producer's decision. It represents an adjustment to his existing stock of capital. It reflects that the currently owned amount of capital is out of line with what is held to be the most *profitable* stock of equipment, perhaps because of *anticipations* about the rate at which aggregate demand is going to grow in the economy.

At the same time, consumers are making decisions about how much to consume and, consequently, save. Their savings (apart from foreign savings) finance home investment. This investment eventually leads to an increase in output, which must in turn be demanded if the producers' plans are to be gratified. For the time being we shall regard investment as 'non-available output', and savings as 'non-consumed income'.

It is quite conceivable that aggregate output, and expenditure on that output, could be growing in such a way that both consumers' savings and investors' anticipations are being realised, but with the population and labour force growing at some *different* rate. The economy may be growing in a balanced way in the sense that saving and investment plans coincide. But *the resulting rate of growth of output may not absorb the growing labour force (whose rate of growth ultimately depends on population growth).*

IS THERE A RELATION BETWEEN THE RATE OF GROWTH AND PRICE STABILITY?

As usual in economic relationships, there is not a one-way flow of influence between prices and growth. They interact. The rate of growth can affect price behaviour and this can feed back to influence growth.

At first sight it would seem that a higher rate of growth should logically contribute towards *falling* price levels, if we interpret growth in terms of output per worker. Productivity increases (or higher output per head) should lower the costs of

112

output and provide opportunities for competitive price reductions. In an ideal economy in which such price reductions took place, we might expect to find an increase in purchases, ensuring full employment and increases in living standards. However, productivity increases do not in general lead to price reductions. (Spectacular exceptions include ballpoint pens, tape recorders and colour television sets.)

Rather, when there is a rise in productivity, organised labour uses money wage rises to secure for itself a share in the increase. (This despite the fact that it is more often improved capital than improved labour which causes the productivity increases.) Since such action by trade unions increases labour costs, and may stimulate further trade union action, prices do not fall.

Within the scope of this rudimentary discussion of growth, perhaps the aspect of the growth-inflation question most deserving remark is that of *uncertainty*. Growth cannot be isolated from *investment*. Investment is sensitive to considerations of *risk*. We have stressed the inability of people to anticipate perfectly the rate of inflation. Is there any reason to believe that the accuracy of predictions diminishes as the rate of inflation increases? In a world without government intervention there is little reason to believe that people would be less accurate in these predictions if the actual rate of inflation were 10 per cent than if it were 5 per cent. It is not the rate of inflation as such that is so important but rather its *steadiness*, which influences appraisals of the riskiness of investment.

The owner of a plant, who is considering expanding his capital equipment, may well make a larger outlay in circumstances where he is 99 per cent sure that the annual rate of inflation in the next five years will be between 9 per cent and 10 per cent, than if he is only 60 per cent sure that it will be somewhere between 3 per cent and 7 per cent. Because revenues and costs are less uncertain in the first case, this may be a more favourable situation for him, even though he perhaps makes a smaller profit on average.

113

It has sometimes been claimed that faster inflation favours growth because it favours profits as against relatively fixed incomes. Profits are an important incentive and source of funds for investment, and investment enhances growth. But there is little supporting evidence for this 'inflation makes us grow' claim.

On the other hand, even if inflation does not affect growth, growth is almost bound to be accompanied by inflation. Resources have to be transferred from old into new uses. Labour must be trained, capital goods produced, land turned to new uses. The incentive used to get resources transferred will be the payment of higher prices for those resources than they are paid in their current occupations.

*We conclude that while there is no* CLEAR *link between higher rates of inflation and higher rates of growth, fluctuations in the rate of inflation may well have an adverse effect on growth because of the negative impact on investment. But the movement of resources is practically certain to lead to price increases.*

# 11

# SHADOW CHANCELLOR QUERIES VALUE OF 'GROWTH AT ALL COSTS'

IS ECONOMIC GROWTH DESIRABLE?

This is a largely intractable problem since people with different tastes desire different things and on most issues the 'desirability' of a particular state of affairs remains a matter of subjective judgment. Growth is by definition change, and change has a different incidence in different sectors of the population. It is therefore seen in a different light by different groups.

The *results* of economic growth can be seen in the way we

live, the surroundings in which we live, and the things we do. Most work is less physically arduous than it used to be, and many people enjoy increasing amounts of leisure. Material comforts increase. There is more choice of shops, entertainments, holidays.

People can choose to spend their time and their income in a variety of ways. This element of choice is central to all economic problems. The *constraints* on choice are reduced as economies grow. Thirty years ago the idea of travelling around at speed, perhaps visiting several countries in one day, was simply an idea. Now it is an activity that people can choose to do, if their income is sufficiently large. Unfortunately, these effects of growth are not universally effective nor evenly spread throughout the population of any country, nor among countries of the world.

Material improvements of this nature tend to walk hand in hand with a complete life-style. Neither the Italian peasant-farmer nor the Shetland fisherman has access to such comforts, which tend to be the prerogatives of the businessman. Ask a London commuter and a Shetland fisherman to give their assessments of the desirability of growth, as they understand it, and you are unlikely to get the same answer. Everybody has his own idea of what constitutes an improvement to the 'quality of life', and it is on this that each bases his answer.

*Less work, more goods, more spare time, and a longer life, are some of the measurable benefits of growth.*

Let us turn from the apparently insoluble problem of trying to assess the desirability of the effects of growth, to the problem of assessing 'growth-promoting activities'. Economists have devised techniques which, while *not resolving the question of desirability*, put at the disposal of policy makers *monetary* measures of the costs and benefits of alternative policies. This technique, 'cost-benefit analysis', is an attempt to measure the advantages and disadvantages of a project. But even by adopting this much more limited view some problems still remain. The notion of 'benefits' is ambiguous. And, inconveniently for

116

the economist, even when the list of benefits has been decided upon, many items in the list may be wellnigh impossible to measure in money terms. The same is true of costs, yet this monetary measuring rod is frequently used to assess the desirability of individual investment projects.

One of the major problems involved is the measurement of *externalities*. Any activity is bound, incidentally, to affect people other than those directly involved. The careful cultivation of a private front garden, while probably intended to satisfy the gardener, may give pleasure to others. The gardener will not include this benefit in his personal calculations. The emission of smoke from a factory may cause damage or displeasure to others, but the factory proprietor will not include this 'social cost' in his calculations.

An example may clarify the idea of cost-benefit analysis. The supersonic aircraft of tomorrow will halve people's travelling time on long journeys such as transatlantic flights. This is a benefit since time spent in travel has an opportunity cost – it could be put to other uses. Other benefits include the possible contribution to British exports and the added prestige for British scientists, whose future may be enhanced.

We can ascribe monetary measures to the time saved, to the boost to British exports, and, if the project creates new jobs and uses people previously unemployed, to the gain in employment. All these measures are themselves only estimates. The prestige gain is difficult to measure in money terms.

Let us now look at the costs. These include the possible disturbances to buildings and people arising from sonic booms; the production of other products foregone by using resources on this project; the suspected malfunctioning of the reactions (physical and mental) of the travellers due to upsetting the body's natural rhythm. (People will arrive in New York for morning coffee, having left London at lunchtime.)

Can we measure these costs, with any accuracy, in money terms?

*Ultimately any assessment of the desirability of economic growth is subjective, as is the assessment by cost-benefit analy-*

*sis of the contributions of various activities to growth prospects.*

# 'ENVIRONMENTAL ACTION GROUP SUGGESTS THAT GOVERNMENT SHOULD IMPOSE HEAVY FINES FOR INDUSTRIAL POLLUTION'

WHAT PRECISELY IS MEANT BY POLLUTION?

*The term 'pollution' is used by some to mean the injection of waste materials and gases into the environment (land, air and water) in a way detrimental or even dangerous to human life. It can also include 'social pollution', crime, neuroses, violence, etc.*

At present, those environmentalists holding an extreme point of view claim that the environment is fast becoming intolerably polluted in all respects and that, given present trends, the human race will destroy itself within fifty years. The debate is well documented, so we shall not expand on it here.

IS INCREASED POLLUTION AN INEVITABLE SIDE-EFFECT OF GROWTH?

To produce any output, inputs have to be used. Resources are therefore depleted all the time. Since almost all processes have 'waste' effects, almost all production will involve a certain amount of pollution of land, water or air.

Two common targets of environmentalists are motorised transport and plastics. It is commodities such as these, regarded as dangerously pollutive (motorised transport emits large quantities of dangerous gases, and plastics cannot be disposed of or recycled for other uses), which have focused attention on

118

the topic. Motorised transport has also inspired discussion of 'noise pollution' and the increasing strain this is placing on people.

*If growth is simply measured in terms of the production of more output, and does not include measures of environmental change – ideas of improvements in the 'quality of life' – then it will inevitably lead to more pollution.*

TO WHAT LEVELS SHOULD WE REDUCE POLLUTION?

Any advance, as we have seen, is likely to involve waste and therefore pollution costs. Even assuming no further advances at all, it would be impossible to actually *stop* polluting our environment.

Let us look at a few simple examples of the sacrifices we should have to make if we were to try to seriously limit pollution. We should have to give up our cars, aeroplanes, oil tankers, many factories, the use of many synthetic materials (and natural ones), cigarettes, etc. in their present form, or we should have to fit them with prohibitively expensive control devices.

Or we could try to find a way of assessing how much all the victims of pollution had suffered (if we could identify the victims), and then see if they could be compensated in some way. But since *all* actions have some external effects and each man's assessment of the costs or benefits of these external effects would be different, this hardly seems a feasible solution. Besides, even the most environmentally conscious people seem to enjoy the direct or indirect benefits of one or more of these 'environmental vices'. *So it seems reasonable to suppose that rather than trying to eliminate pollution, it would be more realistic to try to find a 'tolerable' level of pollution – a level that is consistent with the benefits we wish to enjoy.* It may be that this pollution level would deprive us of, or increase the costs of, certain facilities; pollution control, like any other activity, involves costs.

It has been suggested that those people who cause 'excessive' amounts of pollution should in some way be responsible for the cost of this pollution, and should include the cost in their own production cost calculations. If a coal-burning factory has either to pay the costs of keeping the surrounding environment clean or is forced to change its production techniques

to reduce the emission of waste, it will incur costs in so doing which will be passed on to the consumer in the form of higher prices. If the consumer were prepared to pay these higher prices, pollution might be reduced. If the consumer responds to the higher price by reducing the quantity demanded, a reduction in *output* could reduce pollutive effects. Alternatively, a producer could be taxed on the amount of pollution he causes, or subsidised if he is introducing less pollutive techniques.

Such action would affect the rate of growth. For one thing, making people pay their own 'social' costs would mean that some resources, instead of being used to increase output, would be diverted into the manufacture of pollution-reducing equipment. Secondly, producers might cut back their levels of production to avoid the problem. Either way, the rate of growth might be slowed down. (This might, incidentally, lower the rate at which the world's natural resources were being consumed.)

Clearly there would be other side-effects – on the type of goods produced, on prices, on employment. A careful analysis of these possible side effects would be required before any action could be taken.

ARE THERE ANY OTHER REASONS FOR CRITICISING FASTER GROWTH?

Many people consider the present preoccupation with faster growth unjustified. *Much of the criticism really reduces to a dissatisfaction with what is actually* MEASURED *by the 'growth rate'*. Inevitably, there will be differences of opinion as to what constitutes 'an improvement in the economy's performance'. A trade union leader and an industrialist are unlikely to understand the same thing by a 2 per cent increase in the growth rate of aggregate output.

HOW ARE QUESTIONS OF GROWTH AND INCOME DISTRIBUTION RELATED?

It has sometimes been claimed that growth in Britain in the nineteenth century would have been slowed down if the increasing income had been evenly distributed among the population.

In fact, a large proportion of the profits earned by early industrialists was ploughed back into their firms instead of being distributed to their employees. For large sections of the working community, economic growth was probably accompanied by a *reduction* in living standards. This distribution may have led to a higher long-term level of output than would have been possible had the profits been shared among everyone and consumed.

Economic growth policy in Stalinist Russia was based on the idea that investment in heavy industry must take priority over other forms of expenditure, and other ways of allocating resources in the interest of long-term output levels. People were allocated what the rulers considered 'sufficient' consumer goods for their everyday needs. Consumption was deliberately depressed. People were forced to sacrifice present pleasures in

121

the interest of economic growth. It was only after the heavy industrial foundation of the economy had been established that the consumer's lot was gradually improved.

*Whether or not a capitalist class exists*, economic growth has been accompanied in a large number of cases by considerable sacrifices in present consumption for a majority of the population of the growing country.

*Growth is likely to contribute to a rise in* OVERALL *living standards, but this rise may only materialise slowly, and even then, the* RELATIVE *living standards of different groups of people may not change.*

DOES HISTORY NOT SHOW THAT GREATER INEQUALITY IS NECESSARY IF WE ARE TO INCREASE THE GROWTH RATE?

Britain of the 1970s bears little resemblance to either the economy of Stalinist Russia or Victorian England, but for the fact that investment, foregone consumption, is still necessary for growth. Nevertheless, more rapid growth of the capital stock at the expense of general consumption levels might not now be politically feasible. In the long run, what investment is forthcoming is for the most part *voluntarily* financed out of voluntary savings. Drastic changes in income or other taxes to finance greatly increased public investment are still ultimately subject to the sanction of the voting public.

Some people argue that if a tax were placed on wealth so that it could be more evenly distributed, savings and investment would be reduced. This opinion, however, is not founded on clear evidence, but is based on the view that at lower levels of wealth and income, people use a greater proportion for present consumption (dis-savings) than they do at higher levels. It is also maintained that taxing wealth would discourage people from the effort to accumulate it.

We should be wary of arguments advocating *greater* inequality to provide a higher level of savings to finance growth. On the one hand it is appallingly clear that the effects of growth have not been evenly distributed. The evidence that the private wealth distribution is substantially the same as twenty years ago is strong. But there are regional differences. Affluent suburban communities have grown up in the south-east of England, and mining villages in the north have decayed as the introduction of alternatives to coal has led to a decline of its use. But to conclude that even greater personal and regional inequalities are *necessary* for faster growth does not follow. This would presume that a higher level of savings can only be stimulated in this clumsy way. It is *conceivable* that inequalities could be reduced without impairing the rate of growth, since little is known of the possible disincentive effects of wealth taxes on private savings and investment. If these turned out to be slight, then public investment might be considerably expanded without a counteracting fall in private investment.

*Even if increased inequality does promote growth (and the evidence in terms of higher savings rates is tenuous) we cannot assume that the blunt instrument of greater inequality is the only means of speeding growth.*

These questions of distribution have their place in a discussion of growth. They also warrant attention in the field of state taxation and spending and issues of public welfare. We turn now to some of these.

# 12

# 'UNEMPLOYMENT BENEFITS TO BE INCREASED NEXT YEAR'

WHY SHOULD PEOPLE BE PAID WHEN THEY ARE NOT WORKING?

It may by now be clear that unemployment is frequently not the fault of the unemployed. It may, for example, be due to a fall in demand for the products of a particular industry, or it may be that new, labour-saving techniques have been profitably introduced, leading to redundancy. It may be due to seasonal factors: many people doing an outdoor job may be unemployed for considerable periods during the winter.

It is very often necessary for a person wishing to change his job to give up work temporarily in order to have time to look for another position, particularly if he wants a job outside the area in which he has been working. This 'frictional' unemployment is accepted both by economists and by governments as inevitable. If people could not be certain of receiving some money to live on during this transitional period, movement between jobs would be more difficult, and people moving would have less time to consider available alternatives.

If people are made redundant by a drop in demand for the products of their industry, they must find a job in another industry. If their job is highly specialised and their particular specialisation is no longer required, they may have to retrain in another field. Unless they can find an employer who will be responsible for training them, they have to support themselves somehow while retraining. (This need for retraining will also occur when labour-saving techniques have replaced a man's skill.)

However, it is possible that, whatever skills a person possesses, there may simply be no job available. During the 1920s and '30s, unemployment never dropped below 10 per cent of the registered labour force. This was partly due to a drop in *aggregate* demand, which led to a fall in production and therefore a fall in the demand for labour. There had been a fall in demand for British exports as countries strove for greater self-sufficiency. It was thought that thrift might help to improve the situation, so saving was encouraged.

It was not then fully realised that increases in income, which stimulate employment, actually follow from increases in both consumption and investment demand. The situation was not eased significantly until the arrival of the Second World War forced countries to employ all their resources in the 'war effort'. It is still true that downward fluctuations in aggregate demand throw people out of work.

*Very few people are voluntarily unemployed for long periods. Unemployment pay benefits not only the unemployed. It also helps to maintain the level of demand in the economy by making the spending of those unemployed larger than otherwise, thus helping to prevent further, unnecessary unemployment.*

WHY ARE UNEMPLOYED PEOPLE NOT PAID THEIR FORMER WAGE WHILE OUT OF WORK?

(I) Would anyone who could get paid as much for not working as for working be inclined to take a job? *Any move to pay a full wage to the unemployed would probably tend to reduce incentives to move quickly into an alternative occupation,* especially if such a change would involve a drop in salary.

(II) *It might be inflationary if it caused excess aggregate demand* (if demand is not matched by the production of goods and services – aggregate supply). *Whether this was the case would partly depend on how the dole was financed.* If an increase in unemployment pay is paid for out of increased taxes, aggregate demand is not necessarily increased. Income is simply transferred from the taxpayer to the unemployed. The rise in

spending by the unemployed is matched by a fall in spending by the taxpayer.

However, increased dole might be financed by an increase in the money supply. In this case it would be inflationary.

The national level of unemployed is measured by subtracting
the number of jobs vacant from the number of people registered as unemployed. This figure is, however, notoriously in-
accurate as a measure of the true percentage of the labour
force. There may be many married women, for example, seeking jobs, who do not bother to register as unemployed. There
may be people in part-time jobs who would like to work full
time. There may be people who have lost their job, are living
on their savings, and have not registered as unemployed.

Furthermore, the total figure is a national one and tells us
nothing about regional discrepancies. Since the late 1960s, the
number of jobs advertised as vacant has always been considerably smaller than the number of people registered as
unemployed. Why are these vacancies not filled?

If the jobs vacant required the skills of the unemployed
people, and were conveniently located, then they could and
would be filled. However, things do not tend to work out so
conveniently, and recently, vacant jobs have been mainly situated in another part of Britain than that in which the unemployed are situated. At the moment it is not unduly difficult
to find an unskilled or semi-skilled job in London, as, for
example, a barman or a comptometer operator. But many of
the unemployed are in Northern Ireland and Scotland.

Even if non-Londoners were prepared to fill vacancies in
London, they may be deterred by housing difficulties. If the
people wanting to move have families, the situation is further
complicated by the social disruption of moving schools, finding
new friends, perhaps leaving relations, and so on.

We are really questioning the aptness of describing a fifty-
year-old village-dwelling Welsh coal miner as 'voluntarily unemployed' if there is theoretically available to him a position
as a night porter in a London hotel at the same wage he was
receiving in the Rhondda valley.

127

*Considerations of mobility, both from job to job and from place to place, restrict the possibility of placing currently unemployed people in current vacancies.*

WHY SHOULD RATES AND TAXES BE USED TO PAY OTHER NON-WORKERS SUCH AS STUDENTS?

*Although education can in many respects be regarded as a consumption good for the student, who may be studying because he enjoys it, it can be (and is) also regarded as a form of public investment.*

During their period of study students are not directly productive. However, the knowledge they acquire makes them more productive than they would otherwise have been. Basically it is helpful to any employer to have employees who can read and write; at a higher level, a research chemist will help to produce new fibres, an architect will be efficient at designing a block of flats, and so on. The improved flats and the new fibres can be seen as the payoff of the public investment.

Finally many people consider that *publicly* financed education increases the opportunities for self-advancement open to the less well-off sections of the community.

WHY DO RICHER PEOPLE PAY A HIGHER PROPORTION OF THEIR INCOME IN TAX THAN DO THE POORER?

Taxes in Britain can be subdivided into two major forms – direct and indirect. Direct taxation includes taxes on income. This is also referred to as a *progressive* tax, since the proportion of income taken as tax rises as income rises. Under this system a low-paid shop worker may receive 100 per cent of her income after tax (zero tax), but a company director may pay 60 per cent or more of his income in tax.

It should be noted at this point that the level of income above which tax has to be paid is infrequently altered, but because of the fall in the value of money, money income becomes worth progressively less. Because of this 'fiscal drag', people are found to pay a higher proportion of their increasing money income in tax but their *real* income does not increase as quickly, or may not increase at all.

Indirect taxation consists of such taxes as customs duties,

value-added tax, road tax, etc. Such taxes fall harder on the poor than on the rich, since, for example, 20p spent on tobacco duty is a larger proportion of our shopgirl's income than it is of the company director's. This is known as *regressive* taxation. Note, however, that although indirect taxes tend to be regressive, this is not necessarily so. Indirect taxes placed on, for example, Rolls-Royces and mink coats could be at an extremely high level. They would then be progressive, since if at the same time low-priced articles bore a low rate of tax, the rich would be paying a larger proportion of their income in indirect tax.

*The fact that income taxes are progressive reflects our society's dissatisfaction with the* DISTRIBUTION *of personal* PRE-TAX *incomes.* (The fact that other types of taxes work regressively should also be recognised.) Tax laws force richer members of the community to make larger proportional contributions towards publicly provided goods and services.

129

Let us take two examples of tax-financed expenditures – the National Health Service and the Police. Essentially the State pays for these services out of its revenues, thus making public what would otherwise be private consumption expenditure, or what might not otherwise be provided by the market mechanism.

In the public sense, such expenditure is also investment, since the health of the work force and the safety of people affect the output of the economy. It is possible (though difficult to prove) that people might be less healthy, and the police force much less comprehensive or non-existent, were these two services to be privately financed.

Many people object to the National Health Service on the grounds that they 'never use a doctor'. However, the fact that somebody else has had his highly infectious illness cured means that other people are protected from suffering from the same infection. Furthermore, those in the lower income groups might, without the National Health Service, be unable to afford a doctor at all.

Most of the goods and services paid for by the State are reckoned to provide social benefits at least as great as the costs.

It would be difficult to imagine what life would be like without public provision of, for example, roads, schools, sewers.

*The tax system at present redistributes income to a certain extent by enabling services such as the above to be provided to people who might not otherwise be able to afford them.* Anything that is provided 'free', regardless of income, is redistributive in this way.


# 'DEATH DUTIES LOWERED: UNIONS OPPOSE THIS MOVE'

DOES THIS INCREASE THE INCENTIVE TO SAVE, SINCE PEOPLE WHO HAVE SAVED ALL THEIR LIFE ARE NOW ABLE TO LEAVE MORE TO THEIR FAMILIES?

Generally speaking, those people who have an outstandingly large amount of assets at their death are not people who have 'saved' in the normal sense of the word. We shall illustrate this by looking at the *amounts* which are taxable following legislation in 1972.

On an estate valued at £25,000, no tax is payable if the whole estate is left to a surviving spouse. Tax is payable if some of the estate is left to other people, up to a rate of 11 per cent if none of it is left to the surviving spouse.

On increasing estate values, the rates rise progressively, until for an estate of £2½ million or over, 73 per cent is payable as estate duty.

However, it is possible to avoid paying the full amount, or at least most of this duty by putting money into trusts, giving it away, holding wealth in a form such as agricultural land which is subject to a lower rate of duty, etc. So while it might seem from the official rates of estate duty that money is being taken from the wealthy, thus making the distribution of wealth more equal, the effectiveness of death duties is much less than would appear from the nominal rates of duty.

*The vast majority of large estates are not accumulated through saving but acquired through inheritance. The lowering of rates of death duty means that anyone who dies in possession of assets will be able to leave a larger proportion than before to his family. Present-day examples of the 'self-made man' are extremely rare.*

## HOW DOES THE PAYMENT OF ESTATE DUTIES BENEFIT SOCIETY?

*Estate duties are partly intended to help in equalising the distribution of wealth, and making available to an increasing number of people some of the wealth which has been concentrated in the hands of a very small proportion of the population.*

It has been estimated that over 90 per cent of *income earned from wealth* goes to about 10 per cent of the population. In other words, a very small number of people have a very large amount of unearned income.

Since wealth represents claims on resources, these few people have a much bigger range of choice within which to act than do the other 90 per cent.

## ARE THERE ANY REASONS WHY WEALTH SHOULD BE MORE EVENLY DISTRIBUTED?

Most of the arguments involved in this issue depend on the individual's view of what society 'ought' to be. We believe that we should aim for what might loosely be termed a more 'just' society, and that this entails further redistribution of wealth. This *belief* is not a part of economic science. It is a *moral* issue with *economic* implications, and we shall consider both points.

On the whole, the parents of three or four children try to treat each child equally unless there is some very good reason for not doing so. However, they might give a child special treatment if they felt that he or she had 'earned' it. They might also give a child special treatment if they felt he 'needed' it.

Finally, they might give him special treatment if they felt the whole family would benefit.

The economic implications of such a moral standpoint are that, where people need or deserve more than others, or where benefits given to one person might benefit society, this should be made economically effective. Such public concerns as the National Health Service and free education redistribute resources, but none of the redistributive measures so far used have seriously tackled the inequality of *wealth holding*.

*Support for a more equitable distribution of wealth is based on moral judgments about society. But it also reflects views on the efficiency of an economy.*

### IS THERE A CASE AGAINST REDISTRIBUTION OF WEALTH?

It is sometimes argued that, if wealth were redistributed, levels of consumer spending might be increased at the expense of

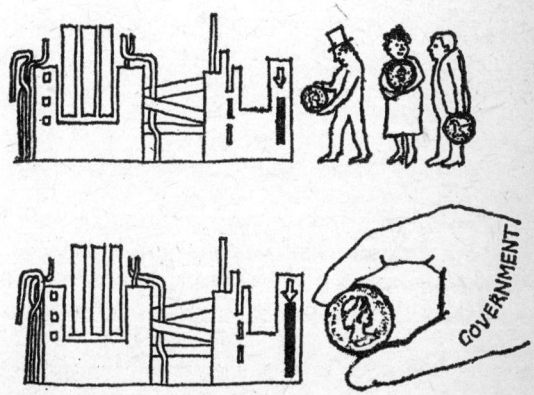

savings. So the supply of investment funds (savings) would be decreased. Since private investment is fundamental to our present economic system, this is a serious objection (if it is indeed desirable to sustain the present system). This problem might be overcome by a redistribution of investment. State

133

investment, financed perhaps out of some form of taxation, could be substituted for private investment. However this would radically alter the economic system as we know it, as it would replace an essentially capitalistic system with a socialistic one.

It is also suggested that risk-taking which is considered important to growth, would be avoided if wealth were redistributed, since the possibility of great personal gain is reduced.

*The above objections to redistribution, if valid, seem to imply that redistribution of wealth would discourage economic growth in a capitalist context. There are however powerful opposing arguments, based for instance on the advances in efficiency from the superior educational opportunities that such redistribution could bring about.*

### ARE THE OBJECTIVES OF TAXATION POLICY ALWAYS CONSISTENT?

Direct taxation has at least two functions: it is part of the mechanism for ensuring greater equality of spending power, and it also helps to automatically *regulate* the level of spending in the economy by drawing off spending power when incomes increase and supplementing it when they decrease. We should point out that a taxation scheme which is most effective for fulfilling the equity desires of the government of the day need not be the most effective for regulation purposes, and vice versa. Similarly, there may be conflicting roles of indirect taxation. *High revenue earning taxes* on beer and the like may be deemed inequitable because of their regressive nature. Excise taxes (and subsidies too) distort *prices*. As a result, *spending patterns change and these effects must often be weighed against the revenue raising or equity influences of taxes.*

# CONCLUDING
# NOTE

We have sketched briefly some of the issues in the debate about the government's role in the economic system. Throughout this book we have seldom mentioned situations in which the government does not play a significant role.

The three biggest single expenditures by the government are on education, health and social security, and national defence. It spends money on many other things, including transport, agricultural and industrial subsidies, grants to the arts and many more. How *much* money should be spent? How should it be spent? Who should pay how much? are questions which will probably never be resolved to everybody's satisfaction. But we hope that this book has equipped the reader with sufficient ideas to compare various answers, to pose his own questions in a meaningful way, and to realise both how he is affected by the economy and how he can affect it.

# FURTHER READING

ROBBINS, L. *The Nature and Significance of Economic Science* (London, Macmillan 1972) (Classic essay on the nature of economics.)

GALBRAITH, J. K. *The New Industrial State* (Harmondsworth, Penguin Books 1970) (Challenges conventional economic assumption of profit maximising as goal of firm, and much else. Very easy to read – non-technical.)

MISHAN, E. J., *The Costs of Economic Growth* (Harmondsworth, Penguin Books 1967) (The assumption that economic growth is a Good Thing underlies most economic theory. Mishan queries it. Also by same author – *21 Popular Economic Fallacies.*)

ROBINSON, JOAN, *Economic Philosophy* (Harmondsworth, Penguin Books 1973) (Stimulating, concise enquiry into the discipline of economics.)

LIPSEY, R. G. *An Introduction To Positive Economics* (3rd Edn, London, Weidenfeld & Nicolson 1972) (Modern classic. Long, carefully written textbook which covers basic economic theory and poses a number of questions. Don't be put off by the length.)

TURVEY, R. *Demand and Supply* (London, Allen & Unwin 1971) (What the title suggests.)

*The Nationalised Industries; a review of Economic and Financial Objectives* (Government White Paper Cmnd 3437, 1967)

KATRAK, H. *International Trade and the Balance of Payments* (London, Fontana 1972) (A straightforward explanation of the elementary theory and practice.)

ROBBINS, L. *The International Monetary Problem* (2nd Keynes Lecture 2 October 1972, O.U.P. 1973)

YEAGER, L. B. *The International Monetary Mechanism* (London, Holt, Rinehart & Winston 1970) (Concise, full exposition of the pre-1972 system.)

PREST, A. R. *The UK Economy. A Manual of Applied Economics* (London, Weidenfeld & Nicolson 1973) (Facts and figures on the economy, fitted into a semi-theoretical framework. The most recent edition is always useful.)

ATKINSON, A. B. *Unequal Shares* (London, Allen Lane 1972) (A study of the extent and causes of the disparity of wealth distribution and the most effective ways of remedying it. Non-technical – lots of useful facts.)

# INDEX

141

# A Fontana Selection

# Fontana Introduction to Modern Economics

*General Editor: C. D. Harbury*

Each of the seven books in the series introduces the reader to a major area or aspect of modern economics. Each stands on its own, but all fit together to form an introductory course which covers most A-Level and first year university syllabuses, and those of most professional bodies.

*Already published*

**Income, Spending and the Price Level**  A. G. Ford

**An Introduction to Economic Behaviour**  C. D. Harbury

**International Trade and the Balance of Payments**
  H. Katrak

**Mathematics for Modern Economics**  Richard Morley

**Private and Public Finance**  G. H. Peters

**Britain and the World Economy, 1919–1970**
  L. J. Williams

*For publication 1975*

**Economics of the Market**  Gordon Hewitt